D0925539

First Edition.

ISBN: 9798835254637

DRAG411 asked each of the performers in this book to reach out to the entertainers around them to involve them in this book that will be printed annually. We offered to publish for free any person that sent one in. We are constantly creating new books and need the input of entertainers. All they have to do is go to the DRAG411 group on facebook (not the DRAG411 page) to simply participate.

DRAG411.com
InfamousTodd.com

Letter from DRAG411

I don't charge performers to be involved in these books. I go online and beg for a month to become involved with each book. Once a person commits, I plead with them to ask their mentors and peers to become involved.

When I created my 10th DRAG book, DRAG Bully, which was my 30th book I thought I was done. The doctors had diagnosed me with onset dementia and I was struggling. I believed it was a good time to wrap up the DRAG411 project and give it a rest. Medication and therapy have granted me a window into giving me confidence to create new projects. I do not know which project will be my last, but I say... "let's race this car until the wheels fall off."

New books will become reality, if you have the patience to deal with me. This year we already created "The DRAG Book," this directory, and the group is working on a book called, "DRAG SHOW" about the steps to get on stage when you are new. It is hard for me to stay focused so I have the performers make it easy on me. There is no way I can individually contact thousands of them. I don't have those files anymore since coming out of retirement. I have to rely on them participating in the DRAG411 group (not the page) on Facebook. Feel free to join it as a performer or a fan. In the group they can post all their responses in one place for me to access for each book.

It never cost any money to be involved with DRAG411. I make my money when a book sells. I thank you for buying this book. The performers in the 2022 International "Who's Who of DRAG" Directory were asked to provide information to help the readers. They decided what information they would share with you. I personally asked them to provide their official stage name, the part of the world they are from since DRAG411 is over 7,000 performers in 32 countries, how to follow them on social media, titles they won, something personal about themselves, ways to contact them for books, a close up/head shot (with a photo credit, if someone talented took the picture of them), their goals, motivations... and so much more.

This book is their introduction. To follow their story, make the time to go online and find them. Do me a favor, let them know you noticed them in this book. Let them know they made a difference. I promise you, everybody in this book wants to make a difference in your life. Thank you for making a difference in my life as a reader.

The Infamous Todd   *Google my nickname. Yep, that's me.*

I dedicate this book to

The Official, Original DRAG Memorial

For those that now perform on a greater stage.

The Memorial is online, updated daily at
DRAG411.com

Abs Hart

Abs Hart has been entertaining audiences since 2010. He is a two-time national titleholder (Mister USofA MI 2016 and Mr. Trans USA Emeritus), model, cosplayer, and trans advocate. Abs was the first King to be put on cast at the legendary Discovery Nightclub in Little Rock, Arkansas, United States and has been blessed to work across the country with many icons from the DRAG pageantry world. He continues to travel whenever possible, working to inspire new entertainers and other trans people. *Photo Credit: Carrie Strong*

Adam Lamborghini

Adam Lamborghini is Nanaimo's touring DRAG King, performing from one end of Vancouver Island to the other since 2016 (Canada). This mid-island King has performed on stage, at local DRAG and Burlesque shows, and occasionally virtually during Covid. Adam is looking to expand and diversify the local DRAG community, because all DRAG is valid. Adam learned from iconic King Murray Hill. If you don't see yourself represented, go out and represent yourself.

Addy Pose

The American Midwest's top (and bottom) overweight, Jewish, depressed, middle-aged, bearded queen, Addy Pose owes her DRAG origins to her mother's closet and her flat-footed inability to wear heels. Having first showcased DRAG at the age of 16 in her native Texas, United States. Addy was next seen performing DRAG in Indianapolis during the early 2000s. Currently a resident of Lincoln, Nebraska,

Who's Who of DRAG

Addy personifies the adage that DRAG knows no size, age, or quality (Addy believes that "bad DRAG" is the best DRAG). Queen of all who ever felt excluded in any way, Addy Pose views DRAG as an art form that should be used to inspire, empower, and uplift. Addy most enjoys being the subject of DRAG photo shoots (her poses are equally campy and proud). Having spent many years within the nonprofit sector, Addy dreams of using her DRAG to support causes ranging from DRAG Queen Story Hour to fundraising for reproductive justice organizations. Addy Pose can be reached via email at coleyconsortium@gmail.com or via cell at 402.314.7692. She can also be followed via social media at treycoleylusk or on Instagram at cwallyc78. Addy Pose is a proud fan of all bearded queens everywhere. *Photo Credit: Chelsea Krafka*

Adonyss Illuzion

Adonyss Illuzion, 32 from San Diego, California, United States is an intergalactic hoe with a heart of gold. A Queen who loves Popeye's doused in Louisiana hot sauce. A nonconventional seamstress with a penchant for bright colors, structure, & texture. Virtual insanity personified. Special effects makeup artist and extravagant wig stylist. A DRAG ghoul who enjoys good times with DRAG sisters. A Queen with an unquenchable thirst for fat men.

AJ Allen Montrese

AJ Allen Montrese (he/him her/she), from Louisville, Kentucky United States. Has been a part of the DRAG community since 2010, started as a male lead and incorporated Bearded DRAG in 2019. Competed in the National Bearded Queen Pageant & competed for National Bearded Empress 2022. AJ has held other titles and competed for other National titles (EOY & Continental). He has also been a show director & hosted many shows. AJ still does his role as a male lead from time to time. AJ has been known to give some class, some sass & definitely show some ass on stage! For booking information, AJ can be reached on Instagram at Babyboymontrese or Facebook: AJ Allen Montrese.

AJ Menendez

AJ Menendez, Master Male Illusionist (Retired). I performed as a Male Illusionist from 2008 to 2017 and had any incredible passion for the craft. I began competing in 2009 and became fascinated with the challenge. My titles include Mister Boiling Point 2009, Mister Savannah Pride 2010, Mister Florida Ultimate Illusionist 2010, Mister St. Augustine Pride 2011, Mister Lake City Pride 2012, Mister River City Riot 2012, Mister Rainbow House 2012, Master Male Illusionist 2013, Joplin Missouri Pride Grand Marshall 2015 (United States). I performed for the challenge of it and for my fans. It was always important to me that my fans saw me as a regular person rather than an entertainer with titles, therefore I did my best to always maintain my humility. In addition, I am also very passionate about addiction & recovery. I teach, speak and write about the topic to help others. I myself am a recovering alcoholic and addict and have been clean and sober since July 18. 2010.

Alexander Moonwalker Jackson

Alexander Moonwalker Jackson is 25 years old and has been doing DRAG for six years. He has two Pride titles and is working toward the next step in his career. He is originally from Oklahoma City, Oklahoma, United States but now resides in Wichita, Kansas. He may not be funny but he's cute, creepy, and an all-around nerd."

Alexis Flame

I'm Alexis Flame and I reside in Queens, New York, United States. and I've been a fixture in New York City nightlife. I'm known not to be a follower of rules, yet I still manage to play nicely (most of the time). I see myself as genderfluid and I'm ok with both she/him. I've worked hard all of my life which affords me both the right and the luxury to play in my own little bubble as a creature of my own imagination. My strong advice, to up and coming performers, is to keep it glam and always be sure to have fun on stage. If you're not having fun performing, nobody will have fun watching! Also, you can be naughty yet still have class. Ladies take it from me, there is no shame in looking like a hooker, there is only shame looking like a cheap one. *Photo Credit: Ruby Starling*

Alexis Mateo

Alexis Mateo is a performer and reality television personality known for her multiple appearances on RuPaul's DRAG Race on Logo. Alexis is a multiple pageant winner and human rights activist especially with Latin community right and visibility. You can follow me on Instagram: miss_alexis_mateo, facebook, and MissAlexisMateo.com. You can book me through Lribookings@gmail.com. *Photo Credit: Kobee Anthony Acosta*

Learn A Term: DJ/KJ
Disc/Karaoke Jockey
plays and manages the music for a venue.

Allure Gic

Allure Gic a Non-Binary DRAG King (They/Them/He) born and raised in United States' own Houston, Texas. They had admired and watched DRAG performers for years and were finally able to make their own digital DRAG debut in 2020 on Houston's "Laugh Track", followed by hitting the stage in the city's only King-based show, "Game of Kings", in 2022. From protecting you from an intergalactic trap to wrestling a possum on stage, you never know what they are going to bring out next. Allure wants you to have fun, bringing a variety of genres to the stage they make sure there is a little something for everyone. Using DRAG to explore their gender expression, Allure will not be boxed into what a King should "look" like. From makeup to fashion, anything goes. As a performer, the most important thing to him is about bringing what you love to the stage and sharing it with the audience. For bookings DM @Allure.Gic on Instagram or email Cheyskye123@gmail.com.

Amadeus X Machina

Amadeus X Machina, Houston's Sax Playing Demon King, has been doing DRAG on and off for five years and started off as a trashy clown queen. They've been performing as a King pretty consistently since the Summer of 2021. They've performed all over the city of Houston, Texas, United States in bars like Michael's Outpost, Eagle, 2.0, Hamburger Mary's, and especially their home bar Pearl and have even volunteered to assist with technical duties such as DJing or working the spotlight at said bars. As a Queen they competed in a couple of seasons of a local competition called Dessie's DRAG Race but now as a King have been preparing for even more competitive projects in the future such as Next Rawk Star hosted by Charlotte Shottgunz and the third season of Game of Kings hosted by Ian Syder-Blake. Amadeus hopes to inspire all queer people to not take life too seriously and to find the spooky rock star within themselves. You can find them on Instagram @rockmeamadeushtx.

Amanda Berry

My name is Amanda Berry. Also known as the sweetest Berry on the vine. I started doing bearded DRAG in 2017 for a fundraising event during a bear contest. I have helped my sister raise money for various charities in the United States. I currently live and perform in Ohio, United States. Together with my husband, we run the House of Berry. I am the father of the house and my husband is mother. They also do bearded DRAG. As Amanda I love performing metal covers by female singers. I think I'm about to head to more monster style DRAG with my alter she-go. You can follow me on Instagram @amandaberryqueen. *Photo Credit: Joshua Driscoll*

Amanda Bone DeMornay

I am Amanda Bone DeMornay, 39 years old, currently reside in Tampa, Florida, United States. I am the daughter of Desiree DeMornay and mother to the Haus of Bone. I had my own talent night at a club called Valentine's in Tampa, Florida and was emcee and host at Masquerade's in Port Charlotte, Florida. I also judge a few local contests like Queen of the Nite and even co-created contests here in Tampa. I am very versatile. I absolutely love the creative outlet DRAG has given me. Photo Credit: Kelly Abell

Learn a Term: "Bio-"
Biologically Assigned

Amanda Love

Amanda Love, 59, from Albany New York, United States. Started DRAG in 1996 in Schenectady, New York in 1996 from a request from a friend. Started performing in Albany, New York shortly after that. I have had some great mentors, Hazel, Iodine, Sherry Love and Meghan Styles. After a few years I have branched off and started my own shows in Troy, New York. I have held the titles of Ms. Congeniality for the Miss Albany pageant, I have one Miss Ferry Street, Ms. Strides, and crowned and still reining official Empress of Troy, New York. Currently I run a brunch every other month at Donnie Magoo's in Cohoes, New York, I have three DRAG children. I mentor up and coming DRAG queens.

Amanda Roberts

Amanda Roberts has been entertaining audiences since 1992. He has appeared on stage, film and television. Amanda has performed internationally in New York City, Chicago, Bermuda, Dublin, and Glasgow but calls Toronto, Ontario, Canada his home. Amanda is a member of the Deceiving Divas and a former cast member of the Le Cage Dinner Theatre. Some of his character impersonations include Celine Dion, Reba McEntire, Bette Davis, Madonna, Shania Twain, Cher, Annie Lennox and John Lennon. Amanda is a former Miss Gay Toronto and has help raised funds for PWA and ACT. Facebook - Amanda Roberts Instagram - amandarobertstoronto. *Photo Credit: David Hawe*

Amber Rains

Amber Rains, of Phoenix, Arizona, United States. Amber started her hobby of DRAG in 2012. After ten years DRAG has been a catalyst for tremendous growth and opportunities. Amber has travelled the country and made connections at every stop along the way. Amber Rains has built a business called Immortal Rains Creations that specializes in jewelry, rhinestones, and other DRAG related services. Amber uses her DRAG to raise money for charities, showcase her talents, practice her passion, make memories, and really connect with people! Amber's physical and life transformation has given her the unique abilities to do most anything from comedy to a soul stirring emotional performance. See Amber in Phoenix, Arizona or maybe your town. Check her out on Facebook under Amber Rains.

Amber St. James

Amber St. James is known for their revolutionary activist work in and out of DRAG and their entertaining high energy performances they are also the first San Diego Mx. Gay and the first ever Mx International Pride; both of which being gender neutral titles in the International Imperial Court System and the Imperial Court De San Diego. They have spoken at a number of panels including the International Gender Odyssey Conference. Not only are they an award-winning activist in San Diego California, United States being awarded for their work in 2018 from Tracie Jada O'Brien for the San Diego LGBT Centers Trans Day of Remembrance. They are also college graduate, with a bachelors in Interdisciplinary Studies in three departments (Africana Studies, Communication, Counseling and Social Change). They also created and facilitated anti-blackness trainings For San Diego State University in Collaboration with their Black Resource Center, while also helping facilitate impactful events and programs through their work with the San Diego State University

Who's Who of DRAG

Pride Center including facilitating a conversation between their self and Doctor Jon Paul for the San Diego State University Pride Centers Queer and Trans People of Color Retreat. You can follow me on Instagram @Mxsstjames"

Amy DeMilo

A Native Floridian, residing in Tampa Bay, Florida, United States. Amy has worked just about every club in Ybor City, Tampa, Florida where she was the Show Director for the Honey Pot Night Club in Ybor for eight years. She just celebrated one year as show director and host for Bradley's on 7th. Thursdays, Sundays, and Wednesday Nights at Beach Fire Beach Bar and Grille for DRAG Queen Bingo, on Clearwater Beach. Amy is an advocate for the LGBTQ+ community and spokesperson for The Transgender Community. She was Grand Marshall for Tampa Pride 2019, one of the highlights during her career. She has made appearances on talk shows such as Carnie Wilson, Sally Jessie Raphael, Maury Povich, and Jerry Springer, promoting the Art of Female Impersonation, and the life of transgender. Amy is Also featured in Jerry Springers book, The Ring Master! She's appeared in a play "peace piece" at University of South Florida, been in a short film called, The Electric Picasso, and recently appeared on a indie film project called, Inheritance! Miss Florida Fl 2000. Miss Heart of Florida 2011. Miss Gay USofA Classic 2013. National Showgirl Supreme 2019 2020 and other titles and accolades highlight her forty-year career.

Are you a DRAG Performer?
Get on the DRAG411 group on facebook
(not the page) to get your DRAG profile in the
2023 International "Who's Who of DRAG" Directory

Andrew Martinez

Andrew Martinez is a Cleveland, Ohio, United States based Trans King. He has been performing since 2006. Andrew won his first title as Mr. Cleveland Stardust 2009-2010; other titles include former Mr. Toledo Gay Pride 2018. Andrew is a Transgender man that took to the stage at the time he came out as Trans. The art and DRAG community truly saved his life. He comes from two well rounded families, the Martinez and the Soul family. He has performed throughout Ohio and also in Michigan. He had the pleasure to be a part of the DRAG King Extravaganza show that came to Cleveland in 2012. Andrew is a huge family guy. He is engaged to a very loving and accepting woman and has three girls. He loves to travel, craft, anything horror related and show his art. He also enjoys competing in pageants and hopes to do more soon. Andrew has a big heart and loves doing benefit shows especially those close to his hear such as Suicide prevention, transgender issues and youth LGBTQ+ and cancer benefits to name a few. Andrew truly enjoys making people smile and have a great time. Booking Information is Facebook at Andrew Hesson or Ahesson6984@gmail.com.

Andronica Glitoris

Who loves glitter? Andronica Glitoris marches to the beat of their own drum. Andronica bends the rules just to the point of breaking. My DRAG is always evolving, I use Andronica to tell the story of what John wanted to be as a younger person. I came out at 36 so I use DRAG to live what I lost. My DRAG has emotion and power. For me, a successful show is when a fan from the crowd comes up and says "thank you" and you know why.

Andy Rodginous

Greetings All! My name is Andy Rodginous and I'm a Pensacola, Florida, United States based DRAG King. I specialize in high energy DRAG with dance and theater passion. I don't let being a "male" impersonator limit my DRAG and allow myself to be expressive in my look and performances. I'm striving toward getting my top surgery and my DRAG family have been an integral part of my support system. I wouldn't be where I am without them and they all mean the world to me. I have always adhered to the idea that DRAG is for anyone and all forms of DRAG are valid and amazing! So, go out and find your inner King, Queen, and anything in between! Find me on Instagram at @Andy_Rodginous!"

Angel Sexton

2009-present day. Angel has and will always be a blue-eyed King of Colorado, New Mexico, Wyoming, Arizona, Texas, California, Utah, United States. I have reached a few hearts in many states, but I was there repping my name and organizations such as ICRME. Always intending to see a smile on your face more than my own, but who can't help not smiling back. Being a part of performing since a child, hip hop and R&B music, dancing, lip syncing and costumes quickly presented no challenge. I learned to knit, sew, crochet and other things from grandmother, aunt and mother at a young age. Mom's the only one with a degree in sewing, so outfits were made when I was a kid were super cool and unique, as I will always be. I love my Sexton Family as my own blood, and fans, admirer's, friends, sisters, and all the relationships that came out of it all; appreciated, grateful and proud to have been a part of your lives somehow. Teaching, what I know isn't my strongest suit but I've done it, taken leadership, effective communication classes and experienced it a lot. So, you'll see me or miss me, but one day catch me on stage.

Angus McVag

Angus McVag is a Central Florida DRAG King new to the scene in DeLand, but old to this world. His approach to DRAG is heavy on the humor with that natural confidence and swagger that the Scotch-Irish are known for. He is a cool cat, debonair, dangerous, maybe a tad bit awkward. Angus strives to bring love and light into this crazy world and is dragging sexy back kicking and screaming."

Anita Betternam

Anita Bettername, aka the Bearded Beauty of Brevard! Anita is a comedy Queen who loves to dance, dive, dip, and drop. She's known for putting on a show anywhere she goes, especially at her local bar, the Twisted Rooster in West Melbourne, Florida, United States where you can find her hosting Naughty Bingo every Sunday. Come for a laugh, stay for the beauty. You can find her on Instagram under @anita.bettername or on Facebook at Anita Betternam.

Anna Flactic-Shoq

Anna Flactic-Shoqqqq is the non-binary punk rocker of your dreams from Oklahoma City, Oklahoma, United States. After graduating from the University of Oklahoma in May 2021, she held some odd jobs before becoming a full-time DRAG performer. She loves creating song mixes, singing Paramore, using campy props, and having fun with the audience during her numbers. She wants to use the art of DRAG to advocate for queer rights and create a better world for queer youth. Her current goals are to perform for DRAG legends and to appear on the television show Survivor. For bookings, inquiries, and weird memes, check out her platforms! Instagram: @anna_flactic_shoqqqq. Facebook: Anna Flactic-Shoq.

Anna Mae Ceres

I'm Anna Mae Ceres, the Cosplay Queen of Cincinnati. Hailing from Cincinnati, Ohio in the United States. Anna Mae started as a Sister of Perpetual Indulgence about six years ago, but now also performs as a bearded Queen around the Ohio region. I'm an award-winning genderbending cosplayer with a pension for Sailor Moon mashups and other anime characters. I have a good following on TikTok where I promote Positivity and Joy, as well as many other characters I have created. I'm also a member of The Imperial Court system as the current Imperial Crown Princex Royale of The Buckeye Empire. You will likely find me doing some kind of Disney or Broadway on stage, whether as Yzma, Scar, or even the Muses of Hercules (and so many more). I would love to perform all of the country. Follow my antics on TikTok or Instagram @SailorSisterCosplay.

Anson Reign

Anson Reign from Queens, New York, United States is a recently un-retired trans masculine DRAG artist who began performing in 2007. He holds several former titles in the Mister USofA MI pageant system including Mister King of the Desert USofA MI Emeritus, and has performed across the country. He currently produces the live-singing DRAG show DRAG OUT LOUD in Brooklyn. Known for his creepy, gothic style - including his well-known rendition of Ludo's Love Me Dead - Anson enjoys infusing his DRAG performances with his background in musical theater, and can be seen performing in shows throughout the New York and New Jersey area where he is known as the DRAG Daddy of New York City. Find him on Instagram at @ansonreign and @DRAG_out_loud. Photo Credit: Emily Monus.

Apollo King

I am Apollo King from Allentown, Pennsylvania, United States. I have been performing since 2002. I enjoy entertaining and I love my audiences. I was King of Diamonz Night Club in Bethlehem, Pennsylvania, and King of Lehigh Valley Pride three years in a row. I modeled in New York City for Rainbow Fashion Week. I also modeled for Pretty Boi Couture magazine in New York City. Currently I perform several places all over Pennsylvania. I owe my sweetest honor to my beautiful inspiration, legendary mother Miss Terry Courtney* and my creator, Jade. Thank you for that push into the lights, stage, and music. To all my fans, I LOVE all of you.

Note from publisher: I don't know if you ever read this from me, but Terry Courtney was the first person that I ever put on the DRAG MEMORIAL. It is because of Terry Courtney that the Memorial was created. She was the first person that passed away from my very first book. She was a contributor. Now there are thousands of names on the Memorial and it is the largest and oldest DRAG Memorial in the World. It all began because of her.

Apothic Said

Apothic Said is my name. He is located in the Pittsburgh, Pennsylvania, United States area. He is not only a DRAG king, but a transgender male entertainer. He started his DRAG career in April 2017. Has done shows all around Pittsburgh, and West Virginia. He loves self-expression, and validating DRAG as a whole. He is the current reigning 2019 Pittsburgh Pride DRAG King. He expresses his emotions through the songs he does with his whole being. He is a DRAG father to a couple kids with his DRAG wife, who he loves dearly; all in their

Who's Who of DRAG

own way. He took a hiatus when Covid started due to his job schedule confliction, but is back and taking bookings. He on top of doing DRAG is learning to fire breath, and has showcased that in one show so far. Booking info: TheApothicSaid on Instagram, or on Facebook under Austin Tyler Bowman. Social Media- Instagram: TheApothicSaid. Facebook: Apothic Said

Arabia Night

Arabia Night is a DRAG performer out of Wichita Kansas, and co-promoter of Kansas All American Goddess/Gent/At Large alongside Candie Khayne. They got into DRAG after doing a turnabout show in 2005 and haven't stopped since. Arabia has also had the pleasure of serving on the board of Wichita Pride, one of the biggest in Kansas, and currently serves on the board of Salt City Pride and Equality Kansas, which focuses on the continued fight for LGBTQ+ rights regardless of gender identity or sexual orientation. Photo Credit: Carrie Strong and Aaron Velasquez"

Arson Nick

Arson Nick is the One and Only DRAG King of Kingsville, Texas, terror of tear-aways, and the unholy offspring of poison and fire itself. Arson is an extreme DRAG artist who's done everything from nearly drowning in digital shows to being buried alive on stage, rising to local infamy at the age of 19. With over a decade of, self-taught, multi-medium artistry; Arson continues to captivate audiences with extravagant costumes, grand entrances, and otherworldly visuals. Despite the often times 'horrific' appearance, the young activist can be found performing uplifting routines to small communities. "I want people to know they're more than the box society has put them in." Valiantly proclaiming the phrase," Do it scared", Arson hopes to inspire people to be themselves fearlessly. All social media and booking information can be found at linktr.ee/arsonnick. [In photo] Arson Nick performing 'BERNADETTE' at Austin International DRAG Festival 2022. Photo Credit: Sarah Bork Hamilton Photography"

Aurora F. Sterling

"Aurora is a glamour Queen from central Pennsylvania. I have been doing DRAG for seventeen years, getting my start doing Pride fundraisers and then competing and winning my first rite as Miss Central Pennsylvania Pride!'"

Bearonce Bear

As I first stepped onto the stage. We all know the feeling. What are hips, what is a thirsty wig, why do I have to put on so much makeup as others; I guess I have to shave. As your ankles shake and you feel them give out as you hit the floor, but the audience still applauds as you stand up. Three shows later, you look in the mirror and don't recognize yourself and question "is this what DRAG is about?" You watch some makeup tutorials, you practice your look, you carve out your first pair of hips, your wig is fresh and clean, your feet finally learned how to walk in heels. One thing is still missing. Your BEARD! It's who you are, it's how you identify, it's what makes Bearonce Bear! So, you grow your beard out, continue to push the boundaries of what DRAG is "supposed" to be. Through the years I have competed in local pageants always placing first or second runner up against some well-known DRAG Queens. The looks in the dressing room and the sly comments you over hear, to try to bring you down just fueled my fire. In 2018 you gain the title of Florida Bearded Queen. In 2019 you

Who's Who of DRAG

place first runner up at National Bearded Queen. Later that year you become the Emeritus of thought (Pensée) to the National Bearded Empress pageantry system. After two years in the making due to a global pandemic you are approached by the pageant owner (Michelle Woods) to join her not only as an Emeritus but as Vice President of National Bearded Empress Inc. I pass this onto those who read this "Why should we conform to their comfort, if they are not willing to conform to ours!" ~Bearonce Bear *Photo Credit: Studio Lot Orlando and Beth Wheatley"*

Beau D. Vyne

Beau D. Vyne is no ordinary King, they don't fancy themselves a King as much as a jester of DRAG. Bending the gender lines both in reality and on stage they thrive on comedy, alternative lifestyles and the unknown. New to the DRAG stage they are melting the hearts in Southwest Florida, United States, one goofy mustache at a time."

Belair Banks

25, Pittsburgh, Pennsylvania, United States. Belair Banks is a non-binary, alt, hood pop baddie. She's a powerhouse who is down to party and have a good time, but to show you at the end of the day that the stage is hers. She's a blend of urban, street, punk, and all things bad bitch. If Lizzo were to have a throuple baby with Doja Cat and Megan Thee Stallion, you would get Belair. With a theatre background, Belair can excel in numerous fascists of performance whether it be lip-synced, singing, choreography. She's only been doing DRAG for a short time, but she's ready to make a big impact no matter what it takes. *Photo Credits: Elliot Bloom"*

Bender Nova

Introducing Breaker of The Gender Binary, the nonconforming spunk fae of draglesque: Bender Nova. Bender Nova was born in Clearwater, Florida, United States and raised in the heart of Philadelphia, Pennsylvania. Bender Nova first got involved in DRAG in late 2017 early 2018. They believed DRAG helped them become more confident solely as who they are as an agender nonbinary queer individual. They first started performing at Mad Hatters Ethnobotanical Kava Bar located in Saint Petersburg, Florida and has evolved ever since. Branching into venues such as Southern Nights, Tampa, Florida to City Side Lounge, to earning their first booking at City Side Lounge and then performed at Tampa Pride Year 2022. They are on cast with the hit Rocky Horror Picture Show Group, The Rich Weirdoes! They say their community are their inspiration to keep staying true to themselves and never lose sight of who they are no matter who tries to bring them down. You can catch Bender Nova Performing with The Rich Weirdoes Cast of Orlando Florida, Mad Hatters Ethnobotanical Kava Bar and more. Nonbinary Representation is important within our community and our nonbinary entertainers deserve a place on stage just as much as anyone else.

Benny Nyland

Benny Nyland has been performing DRAG for just over four years now. He performs at a local bar in Eau Claire Wisconsin United States. It started when his now DRAG brother saw him in a musical and asked him about performing in a DRAG show. He was assigned female at birth but he found his true self through DRAG and is now transitioning female to male. He was crowned Mr. Remedy Event in 2019 and has held the title since then. He hopes to go on to win at least one more title but you never know where DRAG can take you. You can follow him on Facebook by searching Benny Eaton-Nyland. You can book him there as well. You can also find his educational videos on TikTok @elliotspapa. Photo Credit: Amber Hudson"

Bethany

My name is Bethany, better known as the big titty B*tch of Denver. Bethany has been around the Denver, Colorado scene in the United States for about six years. In those six years I went from a boy in a wig to this glam bearded diva! I am lucky enough to host a show called Lip Sync at my home bar, X bar, with my very best gal pal Tiffany. We make sure everyone knows our show is open to anyone and everyone. I love creating a safe place for everyone to express their art. When I'm not in DRAG you can catch me playing with puppies, kittens at my day job as a vet assistant. You can check out my Instagram @sankeyt3 and this bearded beauty is always ready for a good time and bookings!"

Billie King

Billie King is a genderfluid DRAG King who entered the Philadelphia, Pennsylvania, United States DRAG scene in January of 2020. When COVID came in and halted everyone's plans, Billie started to create online DRAG content for online DRAG shows across the United States from his home in New Jersey, experimenting with different ideas to see what suits them best. Today, Billie is best known for his cosplays, comedy numbers, political protest numbers, horror and androgyny looks. They were the very first special guest alongside fellow DRAG King Fuano De Tal for a DRAG King based show in Philadelphia called Hot Stuff, hosted by Johnsy Hannibal Johnson (Hannibal Lickher) and Deej Nutz. They are also the second DRAG King to ever perform in Philadelphia's nightlife competition Snatcherella 3000 in their third cycle and is one of the first contestants on Snatcherella's spin off competition, Snatcherella 3000: Battle of the Seasons. Billie hopes to one day build up his reputation in the city of Philadelphia and produce his own shows and have a diverse cast made up of Kings, Queens, and everyone in between. *Photo Credit: SayTen Studios*

Billy Jean

Billy Jean started performing in 1996 in Athens Georgia and has been a staple in the Georgia DRAG scene, lending his talents for AIDS Athens, The Boybutante Foundation and The Human Rights Festival to name a few. Crowned Mr. Debonair 2004 of Atlanta and considered one of the first DRAG Kings of the modern era in Georgia; Billy Jean continues to rock the stage. He's been inspired by of course, the King of Pop himself, Michael Jackson; a fellow perfectionist. Priding himself on the art of impersonation, Billy Jean's arsenal also includes, Manson, Prince, Frank Sinatra and a whole host of other personalities. A dancer, illusionist and artist, he always lights up the stage with an energy only described as a lit Roman candle."

Bimbo Baggins

Fayetteville, Arkansas. Survivor of the Salem witch trials, Born in the early 17th century, I witnessed my closest friends get burned at the stake (may they Rest In Peace) and didn't come out of hiding until the first All Hollows Eve, where I found that dressing in strange costumes and makeup helped me blend in with the normal crowd. Only until recently have I found that I can do something known as "vogue" and drive the local citizens to insanity! They just hand me dollar bills for simply mouthing the words to music, how preposterous! I feel confident in my ability to slay a crowd and sing as confidently as a bird on a sunny day. Don't mistake me for some "newbie" because your girl's got a fire in her soul! (Pun intended.) I encourage all fellow weirdos and prostitutes to follow my social medias, especially if you like hot girls with big tits! Twitter- @TheOnlyBimboB. Instagram- x.bimbo_baggins.x. Facebook- Bimbo Baggins.

Blake AngelCake

Blake AngelCake is a United States based DRAG King in New York who has been performing on and off for 8 years. He got his start at small pride events in his hometown, and had been working on developing his persona ever since. Newly dabbling in a "genderfucked" DRAG style, Blake has embraced DRAG as an exploration of his non-binary identity, and hopes to inspire others to take similar journeys through performance. His performances range from Country to Punk, largely fitting the energy of the show and venue. Blake can be contacted for questions or booking via email at blakeangelcake@gmail.com or on Facebook as Blake AngelCake."

Braiden Butter

He's a previous Vegas Showgirl, your dancing daddy, the hottest buns in town: it's Braiden Butter! A Los Angeles import, Braiden is a multi-award-winning DRAG King based in Wellington, New Zealand who is known for his high energy dance moves, intoxicating stage presence, ridiculous facials, and dynamic mega-mixes. If he's not testing the durability of his setting spray with poppy choreography, he'll be living his dramatic musical theatre fantasy. Renowned for serving comedic camp, dancy dance, and two whole ass cheeks, he's the perfect combo of saucy, sweaty, and stupid. When not being an artistic interpretation of a man for money, you can find Braiden taking off his clothes for money as his burlesque alter ego Ginger Velour, or flailing passionately for money as a dance instructor. Find Braiden eating all the baked goods, being a flaming homosexual, or on Instagram @gingervelour_braidenbutter_acb. *Photo Credit: Jeff Tollan Photography*

Who's Who of DRAG

Brandon KC Young-Taylor

Brandon is a sixteen year DRAG veteran living in Tulsa, Oklahoma, United States. During his career he has competed in and won several titles including Master Male Illusionist, the Ultimate King Contest, Oklahoma Bold and Beautiful Elite, and several state titles for the USofA Pageantry system including the national title of Mister USofA MI 2022. He has been blessed to travel to many cities throughout the United States. Currently you can find him performing almost weekly at CLJ's Bar.

Brandon Race

Brandon Race is 57 years old and is often referred to as an "old school" DRAG King. Brandon has been preforming since 1984. He is known for this makeup techniques and was heavily influenced by '80s music. Always up for a challenge, he is not afraid to step out of his comfort zone to perform other genres. Hosting Pride events, judging pageants, and preforming at charity events are some of his favorite memories. To learn more about Brandon please check out his Facebook, Instagram and YouTube pages, all can be found by searching for Brandon Race. For booking information, please contact Brandon's manager at binda.cloud@verizon.net"

Are you a DRAG Performer?
Get on the DRAG411 group on facebook
(not the page) to get your DRAG profile in the
2023 International "Who's Who of DRAG" Directory

Brendan Bravado

"I'm Brendan Bravado. I performed from 2003 until 2018 in Springfield, Missouri, United States and surrounding areas. I am known to many as Daddy B. because of my leather. I've lived with three simple rules; Honor, Integrity and Respect (for myself and others). I helped raise money for different charities over the years and worked together to show support for our communities. Besides performing, I hosted shows at a couple of clubs through the years. I'm a former Mr. ShowMeMOPride 2003, Mr. Gay Missouri USofA Unlimited 2003, and Mister Greater Ozarks Pride 2016. It's been an honor and a pleasure entertaining folks and helping up-and-coming entertainers work on their art form."

Bronzie De'Marco

Bronzie De'Marco has been preforming from coast to coast in the United States for almost 53 years. She began preforming when she was ten by entering her first talent show and still entertains. She snuck into The Palace, her first club when she was young, following the steps of an uncle that was the first black DRAG Queen in Huntsville, Alabama, United States. Her fame grew as she traveled from Huntsville, Alabama to New Orleans, Louisiana and ending up as a cast member of The Diamond Girl Review in Atlanta, Georgia. She entertained at some of the most famous venues in the country, from La Cage to Finocchio's of San Francisco, California. Bronzie has dedicated her life to helping others as an advocate that brightly shines. *Photo Credit: Tony Haute Sinclair*

Bryce Culver

Currently the Great Lakes National Showman and MsTeR Keystone State Gay Rodeo, Bryce Culver prides himself in thought provoking and comedic performances. Former Mister Lehigh Valley, Mister Lancaster, Mister Tally Ho and Pump Star, Bryce not only hosts his own shows throughout Pennsylvania, New Jersey, Delaware, New York and Maryland, United States, but he welcomes and grooms young Kings and Queens as part of the Culver Crew. Community driven he also raises awareness and money for current issues for the LGBTQ+ community. Bryce has participated in various charitable volunteer functions such as Burlesque in Bucks for FACT Bucks County, Bingo for the German Society of Philadelphia, and a variety of DRAG benefit shows for non-profit organizations such as GLSEN and Prides around the State. Bryce is a founding member and current board member of GLSEN Bucks County, and he also sits on the board of New Hope Celebrates.

Bubonic Rose

The Queen of Weird, Bubonic Rose is a non-binary (they/them) DRAG cryptid from Indiana (USA). Bubonic is a member of The Twisted Sisters, matron of Haus Of Pestilence, former Miss Merry Snowflake(2015), and former Grand Duchess of The Sovern Imperial Court of Indiana(2016). The love child of a traveling clown, and a succubus. After getting lost in the mall they were adopted by a pack of feral cats. Dancing for their dinner (expired mall Carmel corn, and pretzels) they lived happily until one day, slipping on a gumball they woke up in purgatory. Creepy, and campy; they haunt back alleys, and have been known to cavort with the creatures under your bed."

Buttwiser

I started doing DRAG March, 1992 as nothing but a joke. I never thought thirty years later, I would be still making people laugh and feel loved. I have traveled throughout the United States and Canada performing and doing what I love to do which is making people smile. I just celebrated nineteen years of my own DRAG show, Buttwiser's Bash. I began the show because I never wanted anyone to feel lonely or left out and be a part of a family in this misfitted world that we live in."

Calexus Carrington-Steele

Calexus Carrington-Steele was adopted into the House of Carrington and guided into her DRAG career eighteen years ago by her DRAG mother, Ceduxion Carrington. She was then adopted into the House of Steele by her late DRAG father, Christian Mazzaratie Steele of St. Louis, Missouri, United States. Calexus lives in St. Louis, Missouri, and has been a Diva of The Grove since 2017 at Rehab Bar & Grill. She is known in Illinois and Missouri as "The Hair Toss Boss." Calexus is a very high energy, death dropping queen. Calexus has competed and assisted in many DRAG pageants, from bar titles to national competitions. Her previous titles include: Miss Bistro- Bloomington-Normal, Illinois, Miss Diesel- Peoria, Illinois, Miss Gay Illinois State- which she is the founder. Her hobbies include sewing her own costumes, making mixes and choreographing production numbers. Check out her Facebook at Calexus Carrington-Steele *Photo Credit: Andreu Zuniga*

Camden Summers-Monet

Camden Summers Monet is a transgender disabled performer hailing from Roanoke Virginia he's been performing in stages across the country for sixteen years and is a holder of many titles. His goal as a performer is to simply inspire, even if it's just for five minutes. He prides himself on being a voice for those who feel voiceless and who may not feel they have the strength to be who they truly are. Photo Credit: Scott Church Studios"

Cameron Ticey

Mr. International Gay Rodeo Association 1st Runner Up 2022, Cameron Ticey has been performing most of his life. Starting in middle and high school with Musical Theater and a passion for the arts, it evolved over the years when he made his DRAG debut in Albuquerque back in 2017. After some time performing, Cameron became a member of the New Mexico Gay Rodeo Association and in 2019, he began his candidacy for Mr. New Mexico Gay Rodeo Association. When he was sashed after a long and tough competition in December of 2019, he became the first Transgender Mr. NMGRA for 2020. With an extended reign during quarantine, Cameron was given the chance to run for The International Gay Rodeo Association Royalty team. In February of 2022, he joined the International Gay Rodeo Royalty Team as Mr. IGRA 1st Runner up, as well as the 1st Trans Mr. He loves to support everyone in the community, raising money for charity, and helping new performers find their footing on stage.

Campbell Reid Andrews

Campbell Reid Andrews has been confusing men, woman and in-betweens in DRAG bars, festivals, and pageants all over the country since 2007. Known for his Bruno Mars impersonation, many creative characters, and thirst trap dancing abilities. As well as the San Antonio musical theatre community since 2012 for being the first male illusionist to win Best Lead Actor in a musical at the Alamo Theatre Arts Council Awards for their Role as Usnavi in In the Heights. Campbell is hoping to do more traveling this year. To show that Kings can capture any audience. That no matter the title, the color, style, name there is talent that is yet to be seen. Facebook: Campbell Reid Andrews. Instagram: _campbell.likethesoup. YouTube: youtube.com/user/XDanc3XF0r3v3rX.

Candi Lachey

Hey y'all!! I'm Candi Lachey! My preferred pronouns are they/them, but I will answer to she/her as well. Currently reside in Jacksonville, Florida, United States, I was brought up through the reigns of DRAG in Birmingham and Huntsville, Alabama, and had a brief stint in Goldsboro, North Carolina. I have been learning the art and entertaining for nearly twenty years. DRAG has been such a huge creative outlet for me, and has allowed me to find my own self, through the art. My passion in life is to share my art and creativeness as well as entertain as many as possible. My favorite part of my craft is sharing with others and helping others to develop their own uniqueness as well. Contact: IG/Facebook as Candi Lachey. Email; clachey09@yahoo.com.

Learn a Term: "AFAB"
Assigned Female At Birth

Carmella DuBuque

Carmella DuBuque is a performer from Texas, United States. She was crowned Miss Gay Texas State at Large 2022 and worked to raise money for a non-profit organization. She has been involved with the Miss Gay Texas State Pageant System and its charitable work for over five years. She dreams of someday becoming Miss Gay America! She directs shows at a small bar in Gun Barrel City, and believes in providing a wide variety of entertainment. Cast members and frequent special guests include DRAG queens (including those AFAB*), DRAG Kings, male entertainers, and burlesque performers. She believes that entertainment is a playground, and there is plenty of room for everyone who is dedicated to excellence.

Carter Bachmann

Carter Lee Bachmann fka Ms./Mr. Terri Mann, fka Lynne Carroll, began his career in March of 1978 when Miss Dana Manchester, the then reigning Miss Gay Florida F.I. had the initiative and foresight to paint him as Liza Minnelli, gave him a Bob Mackie outfit, taught him to walk in heels and entered him in a contest. He won. After being a successful AFAB Queen in South Florida, United States, he moved to Ohio to continue his career after a 35-year hiatus. He briefly brought back his characterization of Ms. Minnelli and others, then took a dare and began doing DRAG as a King. To the best of his knowledge, at the ripe old age of 66 currently, he still performs as the oldest actively performing DRAG King in Ohio, thereby maintaining his Classic King status and known as The Ballad KING. Now, he is well and truly a KING, as he is currently and FINALLY in transition living his truth as a transgender man. When not performing you can also see him dressing or helping prepare other DRAG entertainers for pageantry

Cathy Craig

The creation of Cathy Craig was May of 1977 in Cleveland, Ohio, United States. Winning a local club title of Miss JJ's 1978 and Entertainer of the Year for the Northeast United States along with Tiffany Jones in 1980. In 1983 she moved to Fort Lauderdale Florida where she quickly became a name in the residences of Florida's people. Calling Bingo for twenty years and raising thousands and thousands of dollars for AIDS research, medications, raising money for the Poverello Food Bank to feed PWAs (People with AIDS) and many other performances for good causes. Still performing after 47 years. She was recently honored by the Fort Lauderdale History Museum for being a DRAG pioneer of the city. Cathy has done film, television, and now doing only special events and things she chooses to do. Cathy tries to inspire the young entertainers and teach them to respect who came before them."

Chaella Montgomery-Kohl

My name is Chaella Montgomery-Kohl. 48 years old from Oklahoma City, Oklahoma, United States. I have been doing DRAG for 27 years. I have done shows from Oklahoma City to Tulsa, Missouri, and Arkansas. I have always loved to entertain an audience. My DRAG goes from elegant to cosplay stemming from comic books to cartoon characters. Booking information, Facebook under Chaella Montgomery-Kohl. *Photo Credit: Melissa Mooney*

Charlemagne Chateau

I'm Charlemagne Chateau. I have been doing DRAG for five years—starting in the San Francisco Bay Area of California and now in Washington DC, United States. My DRAG is typically ultra femme. I like to look impossibly beautiful and serious, only to do something very stupid in my performance. Occasionally my DRAG involves vintage or avant-grade fashions. I run two shows in the area and own a business offering tours hosted by DRAG artists (Dragged Around DC) as well as a wig styling business (Silent G Wigs). *Photo Credit: Ben Szulanczyk (Emerald Star)*

Charlie Draconis Sweets

Charlie Draconis Sweets is a multi-disciplined performer based out of Houston Texas, United States who got their start performing at a young age at their local church. They are an avid cosplayer who likes to come up with new concepts and attend cons all over Texas as well as a huge fan of the 1920s Prohibition-1950s and tries to center their DRAG on that time period with other performance mediums. They are currently skilled in flow arts, fire dancing, Nerdlesque/Burlesque, and circus arts. Their DRAG career started four years ago at Pearl Bar in Houston, but took a two-year hiatus due to mental reasons and COVID-19, but they're back reimagined and sweeter than ever. Socials: TikTok-devils_sweets4. Instagram: charlie_sweets69. Twitter: @CharlieSweets69. Facebook: Charlie Sweets.

Learn a Term: "MI"
Male Illusionist or Impersonator

Charlie Mornett von Trash

Charlie Mornett von Trash has been entertaining for about four years in and around Springfield, Missouri, United States. Charlie's specialty is horror and alternative DRAG, but he can get sparkly and charming with the best of them. Charlie M von Trash is the co-director and host for the von Trash Monster Menagerie along with his partner in crime and enjoys bringing the Menagerie wherever it is welcome. DRAG has given Charlie the opportunity to explore his gender and his artistry, and discovered through the art of DRAG that he is a genderqueer person. He brings a lot of this to his performances with plenty of pretty along with the putrescence. Charlie cannot wait to see what the future holds for himself and for the von Trash Monster Menagerie!

Chase Hart

Hey my name is Chase Hart. I am 26 years old from Buffalo New York United States. I am the creator of hard entertainment based out of Niagara Falls Ontario Canada. I've been performing for four years where I have performed, hosted and competed across the country and internationally. I am well known for my rhinestone head to toe looks. I've won multiple titles, produced and emceed many successful shows across Canada and the US And I'm absolutely honored to be a part of the DRAG community."

Learn a Term: "FI"
Female Illusionist or Impersonator

Cher Michaels

Cher Michaels (She-Her) is a Northeastern Ohio, United States, DRAG Queen and Cher impersonator! She has been doing drag for almost three and a half years, and does an array of acts fitting any show. She had her beginning pre-pandemic as a guest performer on a digital show, The Baby Shower, hosted from West Virginia at the time, and has since grown into a tri-state entertainer in Ohio, Pennsylvania, and West Virginia both over physical and digital platforms. She is part of the cast of Crawford County Pennsylvania Pride yearly, and well as part of the rotating cast at Baker's cornerstone bar and grill in Mansfield, OH. For Bookings, as well as performance videos, photos, and other information, visit these platforms: Facebook: Cheryl Michaels. Instagram: Chermichaels92. TikTok: Mischaandchermichaels. YouTube: Mischa and Cher Michaels

Chevon Davis

Chevon Davis has been entertaining audiences in the Western New York/Buffalo, New York, United States area since 1982. Chevon successfully sued the city of Buffalo to have the first "gay" themed float in a straight parade. Chevon was the first DRAG Queen to perform at a State University Campus in New York. (Chevon has been the first for a lot of things); from art gallery opening, hostess of Mardi Gras for over 25 years you NEVER know where she will appear next. A proficient fundraiser from the early days of AIDS to Pride, etc, Chevon has no plans on stopping anytime soon. A multi titled pageant and twice Empress. "If I only made one person smile, laugh or feel better about themselves while performing, then I did my job for the night." Photo credit: Heather Bellini"

Chey Boi

Chey Boi, known as the dancing King of Iowa, United States has been working his way into your heart for the last nine years. Starting as a backup dancer for Queens to now traveling as the main act, you can always expect a dance forward production from this Magic Mike character. Chey Boi is here to entertain, steal your heart, and leave you questioning your sexuality.

Chique Fil-Atio

Chique Fil-Atio is what happens when two DRAG legends Louisianna Purchase and Bulimianne Rhapsody leave a DRAG baby in a dumpster. She's been bringing her glampy campy dumpster fire to stages all across Austin, Texas, United States for seven years with her self-produced shows like UnBEARable and toyBOX. Plus being a cast member for Louisianna's Die Felicia and dawning her alternate persona DJ sadDAD for Louisianna's Sad Girls Only. You can find booking information and links to all social medias at EatMoreChique.com

Are you a DRAG Performer?
Get on the DRAG411 group on facebook
(not the page) to get your DRAG profile in the
2023 International "Who's Who of DRAG" Directory

Christian Gaye

Christian Gaye, as seen on NBC OUT (circa 2016) is a Buffalo, New York, United States born and raised DRAG King who has been traveling and performing across North America for the past nine years. He has had the amazing privilege of reigning for nearly a dozen LGBTQ+ Pageantry titles, one including being a former National "Mister Gay United States MI" (MI standing for Male Illusionist or Impersonator). Aside from his suave dance moves and boy band-esque entertainment style, Christian is well known for his work specifically within the LGBTQ+ Youth community. He can be seen throughout New York State donating his time speaking with high schools and colleges at their Gay-Straight Alliance events on the importance of Mental Health Awareness and personal safety. *Photo Credit: Melissa Mjoen*

Cliff Hanger

Pronouns: he/him (onstage), they/them (off stage). Currently location: New Hampshire, United States. Cliff hit the stage in 2012 in Burlington, Vermont to win Vermont DRAG Idol as part of a duo. Cliff continued to perform in New England for four years but had to step back due to an injury. In 2019, they returned to the New England DRAG scene as part of a group, King For A Day in Boston, Massachusetts. Cliff takes inspiration for his performances from Broadway, boy bands, queer artists, and gender reversal cover songs. Cliff loves to perform with other DRAG Kings, Queens, queers whenever possible. Though they enjoy the 21+ crowd, he enjoys creating by family friendly DRAG shows for all or ones that hit on tough LGBTQ+ subjects. Cliff wants to thank their wife and sister for being amazing supporters. Connect via Instagram @KingCliffHanger. *Photo Credit: NTH photography*

Clint Torris

I am Clint Torris, if you don't get it, you've never found it. I'm a DRAG King with disabilities located in Eastern North Carolina in the United States. I do so many different types of DRAG from humans, to mermen, to demons and zombies, to feminine masculinity. I do a lot of conceptual looks and performances, and I enjoy blurring the lines of gender norms and breaking down the binary. I've been performing since 2019 and as I grow, my DRAG evolves with me. I strive to make DRAG and performance accessible and to bring awareness to disability in the queer community. I like to find fun ways to incorporate my mobility aids into my performances. I am continuing to expand my horizons and branch out to more cities and venues. I've competed in one competition so far, and I'm excited for more in the future. Follow me on Instagram and TikTok @kingclinttorris and add me on Facebook as Clint Torris to see what I'm up to. Direct message me on Instagram or Facebook, or email kingclinttorris@gmail.com for booking. Photo Credit: Robert Lukhard

Coca Mesa

Joshua Mesa has been entertaining crowds for nearly 22 years as an actor, dancer and performer. A New Orleanian Native and resides in the French Quarter. Mesa has been honored as Southern Decadence Grand Marshal in 2017 riding aboard a famous artist, Blaine Kern's, Mardi Gras float, "Neon Lights." Josh also headlined in many of the most popular dive-bars in the French Quarter for 17 years, performed on the Riverboat Louis Armstrong, plus many legendary restaurants and Casinos in the city.

Colin Bae

This thaddy (non-binary Daddy) will bring the swagger and all white boy dance moves your heart desires! He thinks he's pretty fly for a white guy, but truth be told, dude is a big softy at heart. Having been involved in the DRAG community for eight years Colin has had the opportunity to perform across Canada. This King enjoys spending his time giving back to the community with the Imperial Sovereign Court of the Wild Rose, and has had the opportunity to help raise thousands of dollars for local charities. Come check out this short drink of masculinity as he makes his way into your heart. Here he is, hanging out the passenger side of his best friend's ride; Colin Bae.

Commander Sins

Commander Sins has been doing DRAG for eight years. He is the first Mister Supreme in Phoenix, Arizona, United States; he created and produced the first ever DRAG show at Phoenix Art Museum which allowed a crowd of all ages to experience the artform of DRAG outside of a bar setting. He is now a local DRAG King in Columbus, Ohio. He is an oil painter by trade and loves to integrate painting into his DRAG performances. Much of his inspiration comes from horror movies, graphic novels, and mythology.

Learn A Term: 2SLGTBQIA+
An acronym for Two-Spirit, Lesbian, Gay, Bisexual, Transgender, Queer and/or Questioning, Intersex, Asexual, and the countless affirmative ways in which people choose to self-identify.

Craymia Rivers

Craymia Rivers, the elusive, strange, and sassy Queen from Kansas City, Missouri, United States. Though her performances are few and far in-between, she is sure to give you something unique every time. One day she strives to be someone people look up to. When she says "cry me a river" she really means a river of joy. Don't judge her because she isn't polished, five years of self-teaching has shown through enough. If you think you've seen it all, she comes out with a mixed bag of goodies that you'd never think to see in a DRAG show. Though no titles have been won (yet) she's got quite a few Instagram accomplishments. With all this said, she also would like to send love all across the world!

Crystal Beth

Hi everyone. I am a young dancing Gemini from Oklahoma City, Oklahoma, United States. I am married to my husband, Bryan Storm. I've been performing for ten years and in those years, I have captured multiple pageant titles and awards. I'm known as the split goddess of the Midwest. With my dance routines to my personality, I'm an amazing performer and a better friend to have. I'm on my way to achieving my dreams and desires for my career. I am loved by my mother Crystal Heitzenroder and my friends, family, and community.

It's time to check out
DRAG411.com

Cyril Cinder

Cyril Cinder is a dynamic and dramatic DRAG King known for his unique concepts and high energy performances. One of the stars of Drag Heals, Season 2, he loves introducing Kings to new audiences. A fierce advocate for queerdos and oddballs everywhere, he wins over hearts and minds when he takes the stage and/or microphone as a performer and MC. Known for producing diverse, inclusive, and electrifying shows across both physical and virtual stages, Cyril Cinder brings together seasoned entertainers with new and emerging talent. He takes pride in being a positive role model for his community and encouraging others to tap into their unique strengths and abilities. Hailing from Ottawa, ON, Cyril Cinder made his DRAG debut in 2014. Since then, he has performed internationally and has dedicated fan-bases in Ottawa, Toronto, Montreal, and beyond. With experience in television, film, and radio, he is an adaptable professional up for any challenge. When he's not doing DRAG, Cyril Cinder is a licensed psychotherapist and works closely with the LGBT2SQIA+ community. He calls from his life experience to advocate for queer rights, mental health, disabled rights, and other social justice causes. *Photo Credit: Kristy Boyce Photography*

D'Cameron May

Representing the dirty South, D'Cameron May is the House of Effort's international DRAG King and costume designer from Houston, Texas, United States, and he's here to make you think twice before running your mouth. He got his start on stage in St. Louis, Missouri in 2019 before heading overseas. Currently situated in Graz, Austria, this King travels the world to bring his unique artistic crossover experiences to a venue near you. With a dreamy and absurdist outlook on his art that is undeniably high-fashion, you know that you're in for a good show if D'Cameron is on the lineup. As a superstar known for bringing a mixed platter of talents, you can also find D'Cameron doing non-profit work with LGBTQ youth to help empower the next generation of confident queerdos. He was also a judge on the inaugural first season of DRAG Me, King, a DRAG King competition series, as well as a co-producer for many events across the United States. You can catch his good looks on Instagram at dcameron.may or on Twitter at dcameronmay. Reach out via email to dcameronmay@gmail.com for booking information. *Photo Credit: Z.M. Artistry*

Dani Panic

Dani Panic -Lakeland, Florida, United States (or Danika Panic under Female Impersonation) is a Central Florida based Entertainer, Emcee, Choreographer, Producer and Show Director. In the mid-2000's he found an early start as a dancer, taking the traditional route of unpaid "hot spots" until auditioning for Vita DeVoid and Franki Markstone to become a full-time cast member of Thee VaudeVillains Burlesque and Cabaret Troupe. In 2009, after the death of Michael Jackson, he would become known primarily for his impersonation work, winning a national award and traveling to showcase this and other impersonations of Legendary Artists. During this time, he took the position of Show Director of The Parrot in Lakeland (Florida's Oldest Gay Bar), formerly The Pulse, originally The Green Parrot. In addition to starting The Haus of Panic, he also helped other entertainers get their start in Central Florida through Talent Showcases and Contests, professional bookings and pageants. Nearly 20 years later, Dani is married to his partner of sixteen years and enjoys a House Cast position at The Parrot after stepping down as Show Director to promote Allegra Williams, working regularly throughout the state as an established mainstay of Florida's night life. *Photo Credit: Christopher Rios*

Learn A Term: Photo Credit
The person or agency taking the attached picture.

Dante Inferno

Dante Inferno is a disabled autistic DRAG King from Bath, England, United Kingdom. Proof that good things come in small packages, he is known for his tap-dancing, singing and camp demeanour. Dante is an exploration of how masculinity evolves through the ages, from suave old movies to today's deconstruction of binary gender roles. A relatively new King with a desire to entertain, Dante is emerging from a three-year hiatus due to disability and can be contacted on Instagram @dante_inferno1999. *Photo credit: Diego Maeso*

Dante Virgil

Crawling out from a realm of vibrant colors and devils, Dante Virgil is a DRAG King amongst demons. Being only twenty years old and originating from Denver, Colorado, United States, Dante brings a more whimsical side to the alternative scene. He arrived within the DRAG scene back in 2018 and has yet to return to his realm, for he has much of the human world to experience and explore. Cosplay was his starting point nine years ago, learning face paint before natural makeup. He takes heavy inspiration from Dungeons and Dragons, demonic humanoids, and fantasy. This colorful shapeshifter hopes to invite others to experience alternative DRAG and become a driving force for young alternative artists. Don't be too intimidated, while he lives the devilish fantasy, Dante has a sillier side that lets him bounce around the stage. Dante Virgil enjoys the art of storytelling through characters. It doesn't only show in his DRAG, but in the games he hosts for his friends and the characters he creates. Diving into worlds of fantasy is his forte. Make way for the alternative artists and DRAG Kings, we have many surprises to offer to the DRAG scene. Instagram is @Infernaldivines.

Danyel Vasquez

Danyel Vasquez is an entertainer out of Akron, Ohio, United States now residing in Canton, while traveling nationally to different venues. She has performed at hundreds of venues over the last 28 years, and currently hosts several brunches and shows in her areas. Winner of many pageants and competed on national level. Known for her amazing and elaborate costumes, stage presence, and dramatics Danyel dazzles her audiences with every number; be it dance, comedy, glamour, or whatever. 29 years in the business working in many cities and states you can catch her on social media @danyel Vasquez

Deacon Slanders

Purveyor of camp, concept & comedy; submissive and bookable — attention, campers! It's Deacon Slanders, Atlanta-based DRAG King and performance artist. Known for detailed costumes, creative mixes, conceptual storytelling, and a good gag aways, Deacon performs a range of styles and genres including cosplay, metal, referential, disco, camp, pop culture, and character. Deacon is also known for his craftiness and creativity; hand-making props, sewing his costumes, and self-making mixes is something Deacon is incredibly proud of. At the time of printing, some of Deacon's most notable performance concepts include Midsommar (shown here), Steve Jobs with a denim tearaway pant, Doug Dimmadome — complete with a four-foot-tall hat and multiple hat reveals, a metal train conductor, and Luigi's Mansion. You can find Deacon everywhere at @deaconslanders, which includes Instagram, TikTok, and all digital tipping platforms. To book Deacon, you can DM him on Instagram or shoot him an email: deaconslanders@gmail.com, but carrier pigeon also works. Let's boogie!

Deandra Dee Paige

I feel like a woman inside even though I was born a man. I feel whole when I dress as a woman because I feel that is who I am. I love when I receive attention; it's me. I perform around Akron, Ohio, United States.

DeeDee Marie Holliday

"She is a gorgeous, glamorous, and delicious diva extraordinaire. She is a fabulous housewife who serves hot tea and politics. She is a fierce entertainer with over a decade of experience in performing onstage. She is one of the most influential DRAG Queens in the Philippines and the proud mother of the House of Holliday. She is incomparable, a seductress, and larger than life Filipina Queen, DeeDee Marie Holliday. *Photo Credit: Jethro Patalinghug*

Demon Daddy

My name is Mori Memento, but the internet formally knows me as Demon Daddy, the DRAG King of KINK! I'm a Filipinx-born alternative/goth King currently residing in Tallahassee, Florida, United States. This is where I first began my DRAG journey circa 2017. With an extensive background in theatre and performance, I saw DRAG as an incredible opportunity to utilize my skills and

Who's Who of DRAG

creativity. I am a self-made king, and the first DRAG King to officially win Florida State University's DRAG Competition in 2018. I was featured in an OutTV article titled "All Hail the Reigning Kings of DRAG" in 2020, ranking alongside some big names in the industry like Landon Cider, Adam All, and Spikey van Dikey. I've managed to frequent venues throughout the East Coast, and have prospects of tackling the west coast in the near future. And my journey has only begun. Demon Daddy is charming, delectable, sexy, and devilishly handsome. His hypnotic magnetism and mesmerizing movements always leave the crowd going wild, begging for more.

Demona Frost

My name is Demona Frost. I have been performing DRAG since 2018. I live in Paragould, Arkansas, but I have performed in memory, poplar bluff, and Jonesboro. I pretty much only lip sync, but I have taken to trying to do live singing now and again. I hope to perform all over the country one day, and I perform glam, horror, anime, video game, and comedy numbers. You can follow me by name on Facebook and ladydemonadupre on Instagram.

Denise Russell

Denise Russell is a 64 (soon to be 65) year old female impersonator from Ohio, United States. I have been performing for 41 years. I was Miss USA at Large in 1990 and Muss Continental Plus in 1992. I have performed in 45 of the 50 States, in over 600 different cities and 900 different venues. I have lived in Nashville, Tennessee and Orlando, Florida. I am still, to this day, the only female impersonator to perform in DRAG at the Grand Ol Opry. I'm on Facebook and my email is drthevoice@msn.com.

Destinē Brookes

Destinē made her debut August 16th, 1995. She was a cast member at Jessie's City Cafe and Celebrity Night Club in Dayton, Ohio. She placed top ten at Miss Gay Ohio America in 1998. She is a former Celebrity Turnabout, Miss Gay Cincinnati, Miss Blu Jeans and has also placed first alternate in Miss Gay Cincinnati America & Miss Gay Dayton America. Performing in many benefits and traveling the tri-state area with her Broadway style production numbers. She is an old school gal and loved every minute of her career. She will be making a comeback soon, so as she always said, "Ladies, gentleman and distinguished judges. Tonight, my fate lies in your hands therefore I am your Destinē." *Photo Credit: Glamour Shots*

Destiny Devine

Destiny Devine is a transgender DRAG Queen from Oklahoma City, Oklahoma, United States. I started my career in upstate New York and then Canada. Now I am a proud native of Oklahoma City, Oklahoma, United States. I have worked in many venues in my time and enjoy nothing more than a crowd who loves DRAG. I love a fun upbeat show and a thriving audience to entertain. My love and kisses.

Some people don't identify with any gender. Some people's gender changes over time. People whose gender is not male or female use many different terms to describe themselves, with non-binary being one of the most common.

Dev'on Ess Lee

Hello my name is Dev'on Ess Lee from Mount Sterling, Kentucky United States. I am a former reigning Northern American Bear "Mamma" 2020 to 2021. I earned this title from diversity and community service through our community here in Lexington, Kentucky. Born and raised in Southern California. I am one out of five Asian Filipino American siblings. I have endured everything and everyone in my life by being me and showing up. I have been doing DRAG since 1996 to 1998. Came out of retirement 2018. I have served as a volunteer and on the board of Lexington Pride. I have also been part of the Imperial Courts of Kentucky, Kentucky Bourbon Bears, Kentucky Fried Sisters of Perpetual, and now serving and volunteering with the Mt. Sterling of Kentucky's first Pride. Titles held within the community of Lexington Kentucky include 2018 Mr. Mary Christmas Imperial Court of Kentucky, 2021 Mr. Quarantine Imperial Court of Kentucky, and 2020 to 2021 Northern American Bear "Mamma. "I am me. I am an Asian American. I am a DRAG King. I am they, them and theirs."
Photo Credit: Kenneth J. Squires

Diego Wolf

Diego Wolf is an FTM Boylesque/Male DRAG Illusionist and stage performer with over 25 years of experience educating, entertaining, and opening the minds of audiences around North America. He is a humanitarian, advocate, animal-lover, and fierce proponent of imagination, creativity, and expression. His favorite suit is rumored to be his birthday suit. He has often credited his discovery of DRAG with having "saved" his life, stating "I am FTM, and I am me. I would rather die young living in my truth, than live forever in the shadow of lies. Especially those constructed to comfort others out of my own misery." Photo Credit: Charles Bailey

Diesel Khaos

Diesel Khaos has been performing off and on for about seven years; born in Murfreesboro, Tennessee, United States. Any genre is performed, but alternative rock is his specialty. Hosted many shows at one point called "King of the Road" and now has a once-a-month Kings only show called Kings of Khaos. 1st Alternate Mr. Esquire 2019. 1st Alternate Mr. Murfreesboro Pride 2021; with a Promotion to Mr. Murfreesboro Pride 2021. Currently prepping to compete for Mr. Nashville Pride 2022.

Dik Carrier

Dik Carrier was created in Lee County, Florida, United States in 2019. He was created as a way to explore a different path of entertainment, and to get over "stage fright." He strives to be better every day, and is always being immersed by the people that inspire him the most. He's the former 2020 Southwest Florida DRAG King. He is married to his biggest inspiration, and DRAG husband, Nick D'Cuple. Dik is often raising money for his community with his tribe, A Haus of DRAG. With an eclectic pallet for music, Dik is always "Ready for Anything." Photo Credit: Blackrose Photography

DRAG Trivia: DRAG
There is no written record during Shakespeare's time of them using this term contrary to popular belief.

Diva Lilo

Diva Lilo Lexington, Kentucky, United States very own Femme Fatale. I am a 38-year-old straight, biological female whose been doing DRAG for twelve years. I am a female who impersonates female impersonators. I love old school DRAG, so with me you will get big hair, makeup, DRAG jewelry, costumes, and full body. I have one national title, Miss Gay United States Femme Fatale 2013. I was the first femme Queen to win Miss Lexington Pride 2013 a local city pageant. I have also won Derby City Diva 2017, Miss Diva of Darkness 2019. I was Empress 39 of the Imperial Court of Kentucky, a 501c3 non-profit organization that raises money for LGBTQIA+ organizations as well as other non-profit charities with in the state of Kentucky. I have traveled all over the country performing at different pageants, clubs, Coronations and Pride events. I love being a strong female to promote body positivity as I am plus size queen. I love DRAG and the people and places it has brought me to. I call my craft femme DRAG. I have a supportive fiancé and family who often come to see me perform including my parents!

Diva Rebel Rose

Diva Rebel Rose started performing in 2009 as Johnny/Jolene Dodge. As a Male Impersonator/Diva She performed at Clubs all over Western Kansas, United States. She helped organize the first Gay Prom in Dodge City, Kansas, United States. She was a founding member of "Paving the Way" a group started to educate and mentor new performers in Wichita, Kansas. Jolene / Johnny performed all over Wichita, Kansas. She was emcee, organizer and performer at many shows and fundraisers. As one of Wichita's Original Divas, she loved giving back by donating time and energy to anyone who asked. Rebel was born when she moved to Kansas City, Missouri. She has gone on to add

Ms. MGRA 2020 and board member for 3 years of Missouri Gay Rodeo Association, to her resume. She has performed at functions from KC Pridefest, Central Plains Leather Contest, The Inaugural Women of Drummer Contest, and too many fundraisers to mention. She is an energetic artist impersonator. She enjoys taking the essence of an artist then adding her style to it and entertaining audiences. Rebel has always enjoyed helping new performers find themselves. You can find her on Facebook as Rebel Rose, Instagram as Rebel.Rose70 and Tik Tok at rebel.rose70.

Doctor Androbox

Doctor Androbox is a trans DRAG King of St. John's, Newfoundland, Canada, delighting stages with his musical antics for nearly a decade. Crippled and ill but frightfully fabulous, Doc will tickle your fancies with his comedic crooning and near-passable dance moves. Doc can often be found at DRAG story hours or performing in queer-friendly retirement homes, believing in DRAG both in and beyond the bar scene. Doctor Androbox released his debut double EP with his 7-piece band the Pronouns in October 2022: Play All the Parts and Fluid Ditties. This double EP is the first album of original music ever released by a DRAG King in North America. In 2023, he will convocate in full DRAG as Dr. Androbox, PhD in Education from Memorial University of Newfoundland. (Photo Credit: CC Dunphy).

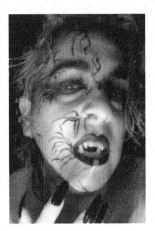

Donny Mirassou

Referred to as The King of The American Night Flowers, The Nightmare King, The Goth Father, one of the OG DRAG monsters and the father of the House of Nox; this multi title holding and award winning SWANA TRANS king, world's record-breaking DJ and trans performer, Donny Mirassou has been doing burlesque for seven years, a DJ since 1994 DRAG for since 1989. He has performed all over the

United States and worked with some of the top artists. He has performed for anyone from members of the US Congress to NASA scientists.

Dr. Rasta Boi Punany

Dr. Rasta Boi Punany is an African-descent DRAG King, who hails from East Orange, New Jersey, United States began doing DRAG in the Philadelphia area. He has taken Pennsylvania by storm winning Mr. Philadelphia DRAG King 2011, Mr. Philadelphia Gay Pride 2011, Voted Philadelphia Gay News 1st Best DRAG King 2011, Mr. Philadelphia Black Gay Pride 1st Runner-Up 2012, Pittsburgh's The Aggressive-One 1st Runner-Up 2012, D.D.I's Mr. Divo International M.I. King 2013-2014, Mr. Pennsylvania Ultimate King, 2013-2014, DRAG 411's first official winner of The Most Popular M.I. in the WORLD, Mr. Queens Empire City M.I. King 2014-2015, Mr. Gay Pennsylvania United States M.I. 2014-2015 1st Alternate, Mr. Gay Capital City United States M.I. (2015), Mr. South Jersey Gay Pride (2016), Mr. Pennsylvania Renaissance Newcomer M.I. (2016). He is a member of the Elegance Family and the Snow Family and has established The Rasta Boi Punany Organization (2013). Dr. Punany has been a sponsor/vendor and performer for several of Philadelphia's annual events and is currently the Director of Outreach and Entertainment Coordinator for South Jersey's LGBTQ Annual event, becoming the 1st King of this event and had the 1st King's float in the history of the Philly Pride Parade (2013). This phenomenal King has traveled to perform shows all over the country and became an International King in 2013, performing in Canada. He recently earned a doctorate degree in Social Science Prevention Science (2021) from Wilmington University.

It's time to check out
DRAG411.com

Dre Seymour-Mykals

Dre has always been his name since he started DRAG eleven years ago. Seymour-Mykals is now a part of his name and he aims to bring you entertainment anytime he steps on the stage. He was honored with holding the title of Prince of Black Gay Pride 18-20 as well as having the honor of performing at Kansas City Pride while holding this title. Dre is more of a suave individual but can change genre's and give you someone completely different. His goal when he hits the stage is to show you the emotion whether it's pain, anger, plain pettiness or even love it's never the same. Dre might seem like a cocky King but in all reality, he is very humble and respectful.

Dyla Ride

Dyla Ride is a bearded lady and comedy Queen from Huntington, West Virginia, United States. She entertains audiences as host of Huntington Pride DRAG events and with her off-the-wall self-made mixes. She is the show director for the Pride board and loves bringing the best talent from local and out of state performers to her community. Dyla loves to be on the mic and make people laugh. When not in DRAG, you will find Dyla's boy half (who somehow manages to dress more feminine out of DRAG) performing standup comedy. She has long been an advocate for LGBTQ+ rights and is very proud of Huntington's 'Open to All' campaign which allows local businesses and organizations to take a pledge of non-discrimination and place a sticker on their door stating they are Open to All! The campaign now has nearly 300 participants thanks to the work of the Mayor's Diversity and Inclusion Committee which Dyla was instrumental in founding. When not performing DRAG or standup you'll find Dyla sipping red wine on her front porch with her collection of over a hundred houseplants. You can find her on Instagram as @dyla_ride and can find all booking info at www.thatfunnygay.com

Who's Who of DRAG

Dylan B. Dickherson White

Mr. Trans USA 2022. With nearly fifteen years of industry experience and just as many titles in the pageantry circuit, Dylan is a chameleon King with the ability to adapt the entertainment experience to each venue, audience, and theme. No matter the type of performance- whether that be traditional dance, live percussion, ASL, or his infamous roller skate routine-Dylan places an emphasis on the details and audience engagement. In addition to his unmatched stage presence and energy, Dylan is a fierce advocate for the trans community, having co-founded TransPride Pittsburgh in 2012 and currently serving as the operations manager for The Gay United States Pageantry System and Foundation. As the first fully pre-op trans man- -and likely the first autistic man-to be featured in an international Andrew Christian campaign, Dylan has no problem breaking barriers or pushing the limits of what society says is possible, both on stage and off. Beyond his roles in the entertainment community, Dylan has earned a Master's degree in Integrative Neuroscience and currently works as a medical writer and editor for an international company while pursuing further education in non-profit management. *Photo Credit: Jon Braun and Molly Belle Cummings*

Contact DRAG411 if you notice a name of a deceased DRAG performer missing on the DRAG Memorial posted at DRAG411.com/

Dymond Onasis

Dymond Onasis has been performing in the art of DRAG entertainment since 2005 in Birmingham, Alabama at Club Quest. Dymond has been performing across the country ever since. Capturing several pageant titles along the way. Dymond has hosted three successful Las Vegas shows and captured the title of Miss Las Vegas Trans Pride. Dymond plans to keep twirling and hopefully to a city near you.

Ellis D.

Introducing Ellis D. The current reigning Mr. Bizarre 2022 and Creature King of Eastern North Carolina, United States. Hatched by Hysteria Cole this strange cocktail of sad boy glam and runaway circus clown has used his platform to uplift others and give back to his community. Being the man behind the curtain of Underground Presents in Greenville North Carolina Ellis has made waves being a advocate for Kings and Creatures in the his community. He's the queer coded villain you love and a beacon for the Bizarre. If you come out to one of his shows you're in for a real trip.

ElliXia Q. Valentine

ElliXia Q. Valentine is a DRAG Sorceress from the Malvern Hills, England, United Kingdom. Now based in Birmingham, ElliXia is a clusterf*ck of gender, blurring what it means to be masculine and feminine in DRAG. She strongly believes that all DRAG is valid and always does her own thing, she is not interested in fitting in with the crowd. ElliXia is a singer, with a rich baritone range and a penchant for a

Who's Who of DRAG

good pop music mashup. ElliXia's set lists will consist of pop classics with a sprinkling of an original song or two here and there. She paints with every colour, usually dressed in something bright and gorgeous. This sweet appearance is contrasted with a dry sense of humour and deadpan delivery. ElliXia also makes YouTube content, usually discussing her favourite records. A friend once described ElliXia as "Baby Spice living in a hippie commune, becoming the head sorceress of their coven" and you can't really sum her up better than that! ElliXia can be found on Facebook (ElliXia Q. Valentine), Twitter (@ElliXiaQ), Instagram (@ellixiaqvalentine) and YouTube (Elliot ElliXia).

Erik Michaelz

Erik Michaelz has been doing DRAG for 21 years. When Erik performs, you never know what song he's going to do. He loves all kinds of music. Starting off in Alton, IL then moving across the river to St. Louis, MO, Erik was a known name. Everyone asks why my name is Erik Michaelz. It's because I love The Phantom of the Opera and his name is Erik and Michael Crawford played him on stage, so it's my tribute to him. I love to perform and always up for a booking. You can follow me on Facebook as Amanda Beneze.

Erikka Destiny Peterson

Erikka Destiny Peterson is a 52-year-old DRAG Performer born and raised in Newark Jersey, United States. I now reside in Palm Bay, Florida. I have been doing DRAG since the Age of seventeen. Started performing a Clubs in New York. I was formally known as Erikka Caine. In 2010 I was a car accident where I lost my right leg! I felt my DRAG career was over. I didn't quit because of the love and support from family and friends. I have fought and overcame many obstacles. DRAG has been my comfort zone since my accident, but since moving to Florida in 1992 I noticed an array of unique DRAG! I started my DRAG, I have competed in several pageants including Miss Brevard County and Miss Space Coast Pride. I had performed at Chances, Cocoa, Florida, Colors, Palm Bay, Florida and Cold Keg, Melbourne, Florida. Now have help in raising money for different organizations such as our veterans, American Heart Association and several more. I am still performing as I go through my change from male to female and trying to make a huge difference in the LGBTQ+ community along with my husband and my DRAG family, The Haus of Peterson's in Port St. Lucie, Florida.

Essence Peruu

I started DRAG as just a live singer trying to make a name for myself. I grew to love all DRAG and wanted to grow into something more! Never let anyone say you are not valid or not good enough. I've had the pleasure of performing in many different states including Cleveland, Ohio, Atlanta, Georgia, Pittsburgh, Pennsylvania and a few other cities in the United States. I have been blessed enough to reign as: Miss Ohio AllStar Princess, Miss Youngstown AllStar Princess, and Miss Red Ribbon.

Evan Bangor

Evan Bangor has been hailed as a rock star amongst DRAG Kings! Originally based in Chico, California, United States. Evan swooped into the Land of Enchantment (Albuquerque, New Mexico) to steal the hearts of many with his boy next door charm, moxi and style. Evan's first performance as a DRAG King was at the tender age of fourteen. Once he started performing, he fell in love with the endless possibilities of self-expression and the smiles he put on the faces of so many. He has always been involved in the LGBT+ community and continues to be a role model for young and old alike! Throughout his career he has graced the stage for countless fundraisers, Pride festival events and even dabbled in the arena of DRAG Queens as Ivanna Torture and even a few burlesque shows as Evan. Evan can be found on Facebook.com/EBDRAG, Instagram @evanbangor, or at e.bangorDRAG@gmail.com. Bio assistance credit: Edward Pearce and Photo Credit: Dave Dell"

Fallon Vain

I used to drag fifteen years ago, and with life and the death of my DRAG mom, Ladonna Spaulding, I gave it up. 2022 is my comeback year in a new DRAG family that is committed to community, artistry, and unity. Delaware, Maryland, Virginia, and District of Columbia area of the United States is our stomping ground. Always enjoy a good show and time with friends. I enjoy time with my husband and my family. My drag career has taken off and the comeback is more than I could ever imagine. Contact Fallon Vain on Facebook or Fallonvain@gmail.com. Our family provides all entertainment needs from private to corporate.

Fatal Dreams

Known as Pittsburgh's Powerhouse Prettyboy, this veteran performer always comes with the unexpected. From the sensual to the serious, Fatal Dreams always uses the stage as his canvas. He is part of multiple performing groups in Pittsburgh and the surrounding tri-state area (United States), as well as a new producer of the monthly shows, Fatal Frequencies. His shows also raise funds for charity, as he is very passionate about community involvement and support. He has begun working in pageants, and seeks to produce his own in the years to come. Fatal Dreams has a relentless work ethic, balancing entertainment while being a full-time medical physician. His passions are limitless, and he always seeks to inspire others to do the same. One of his favorite quotes: "I do not quit; I simply build another way."

Fay-Talie Raynbow DeMornay

Hello, my name is Fay Lana Kawii. I create the illusion of Fay-Tallie Raynbow DeMornay. I am from Hutchinson, Kansas, United States. I am first and foremost an advocate for the LGBTQIA+ transgender youth and adults in Hutchinson as well as the surrounding areas. I joined Hutchinson Salt City Pride as a volunteer in 2018 and then went on to become an at large board member in 2019. I am honored to be an at large board member again in 2022. I joined PFLAG of Hutchinson in 2019 and was an at large member till 2020 when I became the educational director until closure in 2022. I still continue to advocate for the LGBTQIA+ community in school districts throughout the state of Kansas. I strive to provide both teachers and students the information to help provide a save and civil environment that promotes quality learning for all. I have been doing DRAG for nineteen years focusing on philanthropy and giving back to the LGBTQIA+ community. This includes multiple fundraisers for Hutchinson Salt City Pride, PFLAG of Hutchinson, and most notably Relay for Life put on by the American Cancer Society. For bookings contact me on Facebook at Fay-Talie Raynbow DeMornay.

Feather Dusted

Feather Dusted is one of Portland, Oregon, United States' Dancing Divas Feather has been a DRAG artist for eleven years in total eight years professionally. Feather was raised in Colorado Springs and performed for the first time at Club Q Colorado Springs! Feather Then moved to Denver where she began hosting The Witching Hour a Spooktacular DRAG Hour at Blush and Blu Denver, Colorado, United States, you can find Feather in Portland, Oregon hosting Get Dusted PDX,

The Witching Hour and Dusted Dollz, a DRAG and Burlesque Review! Feather says "I am thankful for the experience to be able to grow into a better performer and person every day. Feather hopes to inspire other youth dealing with houselessness as she was houseless all throughout her youth. She wants kids who are to know that there is a way out and you just have to love yourself a little bit more! "I found myself in my DRAG and so can you," Feather says.

Felimena Pussywillow

Born and raised in Oklahoma, United States. I have been practicing the Art of Female Impersonation for 7 years. I am member of the Haus of Kohl and have performed at many clubs and venues in Oklahoma, Arkansas, Missouri, and Kansas. I enjoy traveling around the country and entertaining you! I am the namesake of Pussywillow Productions that myself and my husband of 11 years run. Felimena always says it happened "Just like that." *Photo Credit: The Circle Photography*

Felix Cited

Do you feel excited yet? Felix Cited (He/They) is an Androgynous DRAG performer who began performing in 2021 at Bar: PM in St. Louis, Missouri, United States. They have been actively dressing in DRAG since 2019, yet, due to the beginning of the COVID-19 pandemic, decided to wait before getting on stage. Their DRAG consists of campy yet seductive features and his use of props are his specialty. Their makeup style is anti-contouring and can always be found with 2 black hearts close to his eye. Felix chose his name based on the cartoon Felix the Cat and the overall joy they get when they see other people excited about life. He has since moved to Cape Girardeau, Missouri and is now booked at Independence Place Bar to host The Kings of Cape show with their DRAG dad (Oliver Hugh) and DRAG uncle (Clarence Price). His passion in life is teaching young children and helping to build a stronger, safer community. His goal is to one day host an all-ages benefit show that provides donations for low-income schools and families. He can always be found obsessing over pickles, reading horror books, and expressing his love for The Goofy Movie. Check out Felix Cited on his Facebook page!

Flame E. Morning-Star DeMornay

Flame E. Morning-Star DeMornay is a nineteen-year-old DRAG artist. He has been doing DRAG sense he was fifteen as a way of coming to terms with one's self-identity! It all started because a friend asked him to come support a show. From that moment he seen his first DRAG Queen and DRAG King he knew this would be his passion for the rest of his life. He would like to thank Ladiesman DeMornay for showing him the ropes and loving him unconditionally as a DRAG Father and of course all his fans, because without them we don't have a show! Flame won one title; Wichita Pride Student Youth Ambassador 2019-current reigning due to COVID-19. DRAG saved his life and brought him out of a dark depression. Flame loves doing DRAG to spread love and inspiration to the up-and-coming youth in the community.

Fluxx Wyldly

They're here, they're queer, and they only function in high gear, it's Bristol's very own DRAG Whatever, Fluxx Wyldly! Cohost and coproducer of Bristol, England, United Kingdom's premiere DRAG King cabaret night Brizzle Boyz, Fluxx has been wowing audiences with passion, playfulness and pure peculiarity for five years. Over quarantine Fluxx has been knocking out YouTube sketches, song videos, lip-syncs and a whole host of online content. Fluctuating wildly across spectrums of gender, attention span, style and visible light, get ready for a total mind-fluxx! Fluxx can be found on facebook, Instagram and tiktok @fluxxwyldly. Photo Credit: Diego Maeso

Fran Sparklypants

Fran Sparklypants - The King with the Violin from London, England, United Kingdom. Fran Sparklypants is here to dazzle their way into your hearts and charm you with a smile. Somewhere between a rockstar and a classical dandy, this London based Prince of Ponce has brought their theatre costume and musical backgrounds together to create this beast.

Francis LightningHeart

London, England, United Kingdom. Started the art of DRAG kinging from his bedroom in 2016. Made his debut performance on London's DRAG King scene in February 2017. The glam rock front man serving sex, DRAG and rock 'n' roll. Air guitar expert. Unofficial heir to The Darkness' throne. Iconic moustache. Overall expect a good, fun, high energy show, as if you were at a rock show. Blending the feminine into the masculine like so many of rock stars he looks up to. He brings his out of DRAG profession of photography onto the stage, giving a whole new meaning to audience involvement. Also has burlesque acts in his repertoire, showing that he's a curvy king. Having performed from small stages to, his proudest moment, an audience of 700+ for Europe's biggest DRAG King competition. With a skin tight catsuit on anything is possible. Another of his proudest moments is performing with international rock stars The Darkness... twice! One of his goals is to start his own glam rock DRAG show and bring DRAG Kings to his small hometown. DRAG is what helped him find confidence in his real life and isn't afraid to tell someone he's a DRAG artist. That's what he aims to do ultimately, inspire confidence in others and that there is no one way to do DRAG. Follow him on all socials @francisDRAGking where you can also find his booking details.

Freddy Prinze Charming

Freddy Prinze Charming has been entertaining audiences since 2005. He has garnered over three dozen awards and titles, including four-time winner of Echo Magazine's Readers' Choice Award for Outstanding DRAG King, as well as state, regional, and national titles. Throughout his tenure, Freddy has produced numerous shows, emceed dozens of events, and has raised thousands of dollars for community organizations and charities. He is the co-host of the Arizona's longest running DRAG livestream 'Let's Have a Fefe', currently in its 10th season. As well as being passionate about performing, Freddy is also passionate about education and advocacy, and is the co-creator of two presentations: 'How to be a Trans Ally' and 'From Allies to Accomplices: L.E.A.P.ing Into Action'. He is also actively involved in DRAG Story Hour and serves on the national board. Freddy is a versatile entertainer and makes use of costuming, makeup, prosthetics, and his theatre background to provide audiences with an entertaining experience every time he hits the stage. *Photo Credit: Eye Play Design*

Frieda Poussáy

Frieda Poussáy is the premiere stand up DRAG Queen comedian. Hailing from New York City, now taking on the DMV (D.C., Maryland, and Virginia, United States). Miss Poussáy is here to show the world that the class clown can also be the prom queen. In just three years, I've managed to create the first DRAG show and LGBTQIA+ safe space for the Virginia Tech community, create four shows throughout the DMV, perform at the world-renowned DC Improv Comedy Club, and open for Real

Housewife of New York's Sonja Morgan. However, should you find Frieda during the day, you would be stumbling across a veterinarian, as well as a commander in the United States Public Health Services. Knowing my résumé many ask "why do comedy?" And my response never changes - everyone's life is shit, but if you can make someone laugh or smile, even if only for a moment, you've helped to make the world a better place.

Gabbriella But'zin

Hello you devilish readers, my name is Gabbriella But'zin. I am a native of the great state of Colorado, United States where I have performed DRAG for the last 27 years! I have been fortunate to be Queen Mother of the Denver Cycle Sluts, a bearded DRAG troop in Denver. I have been Princess Royale 40 for the Imperial Court of the Rocky Mountain Empire. I smashed the glass ceiling when I became the first elected Bearded DRAG Queen and Won Empress 42 of ICRME. I was part of the Demented Divas and along with my three fellow performers we ran for nine years at Lannie's Clocktower Cabaret. Currently I perform all over Colorado and have enjoyed an amazing journey that I could never had dreamed of as kid from Colorado. I am sending all of you Glitter Dreams and sparkling nights. Photo Credit: Bob Krugmire

Gage Gatlyn

Legendary Gage Gatlyn was the Nation's Leading Male Illusionist (DRAG King) and has been the Country's favorite "Tim McGraw Impersonator" since 2005. Gage was genetically born a female and "Uses the art of make-up, packing, and costuming to 'create an illusion you will not believe nor ever forget, Male Illusion.'" Featured in the book "100 Most Influential Gay Entertainers" by Jenettha Baines, he was also voted best DRAG King of 2005 by Jacksonville, Florida,

Who's Who of DRAG

United States. He captured thirteen Titles in his career, and he was the most 'booked' DRAG King in history for fifteen years (over 130 venues), and was responsible for the growth of DRAG Kings and Male Illusion by the hundreds since he hit the stage back in '03. His National Titles include Mister Gay United States, MI (Male Illusionist) 2012, 'Viewer's Choice' National EOY MI 2006, Mr. Gay USA, FMI 2006, and 10 other state and local titles. Gage is known in the King world, for "Raising the Bar" by exposing a new kind of 'Kinging' and encouraging more realistic use of facial hair, realistic concealment of binding, packing, chest/face contour make-up, and overall pride in visual performance. Gage is also an avid Transgender advocate and Vice President of the Gatlyn Dame Group, a support group for trans/non-binary individuals and allies. Gage is/was the promoter for: Master Male Illusionist - MI Intl Contest –Founder *2010; & Mister USofA, MI – Creator/Promoter - 2007-2009, 2014 – 2021. "Why reach for the moon, when you can touch the stars." Gage Gatlyn *Photo Credit: Jenna Bowen.*

Galaxy Rose

Galaxy Rose (she/they) is just as her name suggests, a celestial flower layered with petals and thorns. A versatile queen, with a passion for singing live. Based in London, Ontario, Canada; she has graced many of the local stages and is known for her diverse looks. From edgy, punky and raw alt DRAG, to glamourous silhouettes. She is also an advocate for LGBTQ2A+ and BIPOC communities and strives to use her platform to shed light on those who need it most. She is a skilled host, and is known in her community to be kind, witty and amicable with a dry sense of humour. She aspires to make every moment count, to fold people into her world and show them how beautiful they are. DRAG, for her, is an immersion into all the things she loves. Fashion, music, dance, art and her community. She considers herself a mosaic of the people she draws inspiration from. "Let's light up the sky together" she's everybody's gal, Galaxy Rose! Facebook: QueenGalaxy Rose. Instagram: GalaxyRoseOfficial. Email for bookings: Galaxyroseofficial@hotmail.com

Galaxÿ

Born in 1994. The one and only Caymanian Queen, The Master Bedazzler and Miss Tampa Pride 2022. Galaxÿ has been doing DRAG since 2012 and has overcome many struggles and obstacles. He believes that everyone in their life is a star of the Galaxÿ and everyone will have their chance to shine. Type 1 diabetic, fighting the good fight, and got their start in the LGBT Community through volunteer work with PFLAG Tampa, The Homeless Coalition and Tampa Pride. Stay Blessed, Stay Beautiful and Keep Shining! Photo Credit: Erika Wagner, The DRAG Photographer

Gator Dunn

I am the Character King. I am 47 years young. At the time of this photo, I have been DRAG entertaining for fourteen months. I first stepped onstage during an open talent night and haven't stopped since. I hope to make the audience smile and have a fun time with me. I am based out of Oklahoma City, Oklahoma, United States. We are a small but mighty community with a big heart. "Book more Kings!"

Every October we collect the information posted in these books from the DRAG performers. They provide us the information. If someone is missing, it is because they have not sent us their biography and picture... yet. Each book we hope to double in size. This is the first "International Who's Who of DRAG" book.

Gemini Skye

36, Colorado Springs, Colorado, United States. Gemini has been in the DRAG world for 9 years. During this time, they've been able to make a name for themselves throughout the front range of Colorado. Becoming a Hosting and producing legend with some of Colorado Springs favorite Burlesque and DRAG shows under her belt. Having 10 children along the way, she has curated each of them to their own specific niche; birthing a top tier family of entertainers with the Haus of Skye. Charity work is never far away, Donating her time and talents for last 5 years to Dragutante & UCPPE. In her presence, you can feel her heart beam from within. She is mom. She is beauty. She is grace, all with a beard on her face.

George Not-Strait

George Not-Strait is a Denver, Colorado, United States DRAG King who loves to dabble in all forms of DRAG, from alternative to draglesque to country. They love to play with gender and push their comfort zone. DRAG has helped him in his gender journey. They produce an open-stage show in Denver, called StageFluid.

Ginger B Snapps

My name is Ginger B Snapps and currently live and perform in Ft. Myers, Florida, United States. I was a late arrival to the DRAG community, starting at the age of 44, and have been performing for the past eight years. I am married to an amazing man that I met while performing and have three beautiful step daughters. I had always been a fan of the art of DRAG and female illusion, but never thought I had what it took to do what I admired so much. I bit the bullet and took the leap and have turned it into a full-time career. DRAG has given me a voice that I have used to bring awareness to causes near and dear to me and my community. I have had the opportunity to work with some amazing organizations and charities and was appointed to a seat on the board of directors for the McGregor Clinic, our local HIV/AIDS clinic, where I have served for the last four years. I continue to entertain and perform in South West Florida as the Entertainment Director at Eden, A Show Bar.

Gingerella

Gingerella, A Fairies Tale: A newbie to the DRAG world, but not to the stage. Gingerella hales from, Medina, Ohio, United States. Gingerella was born during covid, performing evening "Cocktails and Cabaret" for her Facebook viewers. Gingerella spent many days cooking up soups for the elderly during covid, and has been working on starting "Meals on Heels" for the HIV shut-ins in her community. Currently, she has started her "DRAG me to Dinner" where she sings her heart out to bring joy and love. Happily married to her husband, Anderfella, they work towards opening up the minds of others. *Photo Credit: Ian Argo.*

Goo

Boo it's Goo how are you? Goo is a spooky King that has been haunting the clubs of Melbourne, Australia since 2019. He's been described as a fever dream, sleep paralysis demon and the Babadook if he liked classic rock and jazz. He's a lot like your bogan uncle at a barbecue who loves 1970s Dad Rock except with the added bonus of being undead. Weird, wacky and wonderful, Goo is your friendly neighbourhood ghoul who's here to have a good, gruesome time! Catch him on Instagram @itmegoo. Goo on Youtube and on Facebook as itmegoo. Photo Credit: Moxie Delite

Gotrix Heyoka Michel

Gotrix Heyoka Michel is a DRAG clown that just loves to make people smile and laugh. He is fun, energetic, and full of dumb puns. His performances can range anywhere from fun and jumpy to scary and creepy. He is from the small town of Basile, Louisiana, United States though he resides in Spokane, Washington. He holds the title of Imperial Knight #46 of the Imperial Sovereign Court of Spokane. He has been serving the community since 2017 and plans to continue for many more years.

Are you a DRAG Performer?
Get on the DRAG411 group on facebook
(not the page) to get your DRAG profile in the
2023 International "Who's Who of DRAG" Directory

Grandma Pearl

I'm an old circus performer from years ago. I can't remember how long I have been doing DRAG. I was around 16 or so, traveling on a small show when the owner of the show came to my daddy and told him that the Trapeze lady hurt herself and couldn't perform. At that time, I was practicing trap, so they took me to wardrobe for a costume to perform in her place! The audience had no idea. I was arrested a few times in DRAG because I didn't have three articles of men's clothes underneath my dress. DRAG has come a long way since those days. I do comedy DRAG now. I put all of what I learned as a clown from timing to sewing etc. All I can say now after all of these years, I'm still living my dream!

Grei Culver

Grei Culver has been a part of the Culver House for two years, performing across Pennsylvania, New Jersey and Delaware, United States. Grei is an androgynous performer who pushes gender boundaries and enjoys powerful acts that include the use of sign language and DEI messages. Grei has participated in various volunteer functions such as Burlesque in Bucks for FACT Bucks County and Pride events with Culver Entertainment and New Hope Celecrates.

It's time to check out
DRAG411.com

Grimm Foxx

Grimm Foxx sunk his teeth into the pulse of the Des Moines, Iowa, United States nightlife scene in the summer of 2021, and necks haven't been safe since. In that time, he has been a nominee in the East Village DRAG Awards 2021, Cityviews Best of Des Moines 2022 DRAG King category, and a finalist in the first ever Saddle Ghoul Competition 2021. Spooky, alternative, and a little 2006 emo, Grimm hopes to inspire alt creatures of the night everywhere. @grimmfoxx

Ground Zero

Ground Zero is a Transgender, South Florida, United States King. A proud member of the Haus of Chambers and as of October 2022 he'll be performing DRAG for one year. For him, DRAG became a way of finding himself and his comfort. Leaning towards Punk and rock when performing. His DRAG tends to fall in a mix of religious types, rockabilly fashion, cosplay and Punk styles. Every show he comes out and gives 100%. High energy performances, and most unique, Fire. Proud to represent the alternative community in South Florida and bring the Niche of fire and flow to the world of DRAG. You can find him on Instagram and Facebook by searching for @GroundZeroCosplay

Contact DRAG411 if you notice a name of a deceased DRAG performer missing on the DRAG Memorial posted at DRAG411.com/

Hannibal Lickher

Hannibal Lickher is your current reigning Mr. Philly DRAG King. As a Non-Binary (they/them) Queer DRAG King they're paving the way for future DRAG here in Philadelphia, Pennsylvania, United States. Co-Producing in Philadelphia with the only monthly DRAG King show in the tri-state area alongside Deej Nutz and running Haus of Lickher productions out of Franky Bradley's featuring DRAG, Burlesque and various performance art they hope to create an experience at each show. With many years under their belt in the DRAG scene, Hannibal has only been around for about 6 years now and hopes to continue to create a stage for all DRAG King's, Masc & DRAG Royalty. With the tagline 'They're a bit of tramp but mostly a vamp', they hope to woo you into submission. *Photo Credit: Jonathan Hernandez*

Harley Q Lunár

Hello, It's the Princette of the Haus of Cavalli, The Princette of Chaos, the Duchess of Kansas City. The one and only Mx. Harley Q. Lunár (She/Her/They/Them). I am from Kansas City, Missouri, United States. Born and raised. Harley comes from Harley Quinn. A world of Chaos, Anger, Sadness, Loyalty and Fun. I describe her as the Hood Clown. She was born from my heartache from past romantic relationships. She is my expression of the pain I felt through breakups and also from the attempts of my life. I consider her as a nonbinary character like myself. She can do masculine and also feminine. Blessed on the microphone, and with crazy story telling. Harley is one that makes you think, and grab your attention through emotions. I would love to take her to America's Bearded Queen, National Monster Extreme, and National Bearded Empress. If I really want, I am looking into Dragula as well. She is fairly new, but I know she will grab your attention. You can follow her on Facebook Harley Q Lunár.

Hayden Lee Sunshine

Hayden Lee Sunshine is a newer king in the United States. He is hitting hit year-old birthday on July 12, 2022. Hayden likes to perform for everyone. He is a King who likes to put smiles on faces, and make you crave for more. Hayden brings personality, emotion, and a fun time. Hayden just won his first title as King of Kansas City Pride 2022. Hayden is dedicated to keep his DRAG growing and reaching big dreams and goals! *Photo Credit: Sandy Woodson*

Heather-Marie TaterSalad Thomas

Heather-Marie TaterSalad Thomas is a thirty something trans entertainers from Baltimore Maryland. She has over a decade of experience in DRAG and nearly twenty years in nightlife in general. She has held several local titles in Baltimore, most recently winning the title of Miss Mixers 2022. She's working now towards being an advocate for sober and dry spaces with in the DRAG community and the greater queer community.

Heidi Banks

Heidi Banks was born on a dark, cold night in the mountains of Nova Scotia, Canada to a sleuth of Bears. One night, an old mountain man, looking like a swollen ass Santa Claus, stumbled across her in a cave while her Bears were out hunting. He took her in and called her Heidi. Raised on a diet of whiskey and jerky, he taught her to be stunning, sickening, and most of all, c.u.n.t., which lead her all the way to the Heart of America. She is a former Queen of KC Gay Pride and Miss Gay KC

America. But mostly, she just a bearded baddie with a fatty from Kansas City who wants to share her DRAG with the world. follow on insta @heidinaomibanks

Heidi Salami

Heidi Salami is an effervescent and ever-changing club kid inspired DRAG artist. She was born in Fort Smith, Arkansas, United States. She was brought to life in Little Rock, Arkansas. She also called Asbury Park, New York City, Chicago, and Oregon home. With six years in the profession, and many more to hopefully come - she has most identified with the title of heroine chic fashion wench of Arkansas, but give it a day and it may change. We love a good brand! Hence my "muggle" job in marketing and advertising. Heidi 1.0 forever. @heidsalami on Instagram, and all the other socials. Let's connect! Isn't that the point of life? If not, tell me what you think is, and let's make some magic! Follow @heidisalami - photography by Heidi Salami herself.

Henlo Bullfrog

An FX stunt King and real-life art superhero whose award-winning body artistry blends stagecraft, costuming, and special effects to create such signature moves as quick-change makeup transformations; invisible ultraviolet reveals; and tearing his own face off. DRAG venues report that sightings of Henlo Bullfrog may involve stage blood, missing time, and blurriness. *Photo Credit: Joe Mac Creative*

Check out the book
DRAG Bully!
From DRAG411

Homer Neurotic

He's blue in more ways than one, he's Wellington's resident sad boy, give it up for Homer Neurotic! Homer Neurotic is a multi-award-winning campy DRAG King hailing from Windy Wellington in Aotearoa, New Zealand. His acts are renowned for their silly storytelling, ambitious reveals and genuine heart. When he's not bringing the bangers, you'll find him behind the mic emceeing up a storm. He loves to use humour, levity and random trivia so you leave with a smile on your face and a tug on your heartstring. In his relatively short time on stage, Homer has taken home a few of Wellington's newest performing titles, including being awarded the Den of Thurst's first Lip Sync Assassin (2020), Kelly Fornia's first Evolution Grand Champion and People's Choice (2021) and Kelly Fornia's first Ultimate DRAG Royale Co-Champion (2021), a title he shares with Wellington's Scottish Daddy and local legend, Willy SmacknTush. You can keep up with Homer's antics on Facebook and Instagram (@homerneurotic). *Photo Credit: Jeff Tollan Photography.*

House of 86

Hailing from Aotearoa, New Zealand, House of 86 is a Pacific Island and Māori power player. In 1986, two very important things happened in Aotearoa - House of 86 was born, and the Homosexual Law Reform was passed where being Gay in New Zealand was no longer considered illegal. "86" has been lucky enough to always live in a homosexually liberated country, but understands it important to acknowledge who and what has come before. Exploring aspects of Gender Identity, Pacific Values and Pop Culture, House of 86 provides a unique perspective to the audience, but always with a twist and a chuckle. Afterall, we Pacific Islanders know a message is best delivered with a laugh. Their current stage work continues to deconstruct two important religious figures in Pacific Island culture - Jesus and Colonel Sanders. If you're ever in Aotearoa, be sure to catch this King serving up your dinner at Caluzzi Cabaret for boss lady Kita Mean, Winner of Season 1, DRAG Race Down Under, and follow them on Instagram @house.eighty.6 .

Hunta Downe

Hunta Downe a native of New Orleans. He enjoys the quiet living of Monroe, Louisiana. He the 1st Mister Louisiana USofA MI. Hunta also held the titles of Mister Arkansas USofA MI Classic and Mister Cenla Pride of Central Louisiana, Louisiana. He is the former pageant co-promoter for Mister Louisiana USofA MI, Miss Louisiana USofA Diva, former co-promoter of Mr. Gay Louisiana America, Mr. Gay Louisiana USofA and USofA at Large. Case worker by day; DRAG King by night.

Idle King

Idle King is an autistic DRAG King in Auburn, Alabama, United States. They started doing DRAG on TikTok back in 2020 but they didn't hit the stage until April of 2021. Their journey as a DRAG King has been closely tied to their exploration of being genderfluid. That's why they frequently go from pretty in pink to space raccoon to cosplay villain vibes in a single weekend. They call themself a King while they float freely along the gender spectrum. They are the first runner up for both Mx Pride on the Plains 2022 and Mx East Alabama Newcomer 2022, which are the first two pageants in the state of Alabama to offer the Mx category. They intend to do more pageants but they don't have any interest in limiting their DRAG to strictly masculine or feminine. This means they only feel comfortable competing when the Mx category is offered. They have found an incredibly supportive community in Auburn with fellow Kings and nonbinary performers taking the stage regularly. Idle wouldn't have made the progress they have without that support and opportunities to grow as a performer. You can find them on Instagram at @The_Idle_King4. Photo Credit: Photography by Fox.

Iman

Hey y'all! I'm Iman (They/Them, She/Her), and I'm originally from San Antonio, Texas, United States but now reside in Oakland, California. I came into the DRAG scene in the early 2000s just fell in love. I'm a BIPOC, Deaf, Queer Queen who uses ASL (American Sign Language) in many of my performances. My style of DRAG is inspired from many categories, but is mostly known for invigorating dance, high octane beats, and precise choreography. I've been involved in several community programs, and have performed for numerous charity events. I was crowned Princess of The Ducal Court in 2021, and continue to encourage, uplift, and inspire and entertain. I have had the honor to come a long line of fabulous and Legendary Queen houses. My art is always growing. I'm constantly seeking ways to improve, evolve, all while trying to educate and incorporate the many intersections that make me, "me." Instagram: Freespeak84. Photo Credit: Darrel Thigpen

Immalee Ess Cook

Bio female. Hometown Mount Sterling, Kentucky. United States. Related to Dev'on Ess Lee (Cousin). She is a firecracker that wins everyone's heart. She can be a demon at heart but a bit lavishing when it comes to her sexuality. She does not fear her body image. She is also part of the Imperial Court of Kentucky, The Kentucky Fried Sisters of Perpetual, Capital Pride of Frankfort Kentucky, Kentucky Bourbon Bears, Black Pride of Kentucky, Lexington Pride, and more to come. She has been in prior pageants including Imperial Court of Kentucky

Miss Derby Pride, Diva of Darkness, Miss Bar Complex, and Miss Firecracker. She does not have a title but all she likes to do is perform and have fun.

Infinity LaVey Adonis

Hi, my name is Infinity LaVey Adonis and when this is written I would have been doing DRAG for almost five years in College Station and Bryan, Texas, United States! I started DRAG as a way to inspire people around me and also to help me grow as a person and an individual. I helped build up a community in a very conservative part of Texas and will continue to help grow this community. My DRAG is a little bit of everything from glamour pageant styles to dark horror creatures. I love the art of DRAG and wouldn't be the person I am without it! If you want to follow my journey even more you can always follow me on my socials. Instagram: @infinitylavey.

Irish Lashez

Irish Lashes (they/them) is here to preposition you under, on top of, and between the gender spectrum. Blurring lines of gender expression through DRAG and burlesque since 2017, Irish Lashes has an act for all occasions, from femmes in space to masculine recycling rituals to nerdy tributes. In 2018 they started producing burlesque shows under the label Irish Lashes Productions. Irish's favorite part of DRAG is that it has a history in letting marginalized queer people explore themselves outside the hetero- and cis-normative views of mainstream society. Their goal is to continue adding to that rich history through their own performances and by prioritizing marginalized queer performers in their productions. Currently based in Seattle, Washington, United States, you can find out where Irish is live or virtually by following them on their website www.IrishLashes.com. *Photo Credit: Keith Johnson*

irishimo

irishimo (all small font) is a transforming DRAG Monster and Goblin. They or He in or out of DRAG. They live in Pueblo Colorado, United States, and love to travel to shows and meet new creatures! They make most of their costumes or alter them for custom design. Though, they do love to commission other artists when they can. They have always had a passion for theater, classical film, and art. They used to work as a clown doing face painting, caricatures, entertainment, and occasional mascot and cosplay appearances for birthday parties and events. Their dream is to inspire others to be who they want to be, even if it is the monsters from the imagination. DRAG is limitless. They have always loved makeup, sewing and special effects prosthetics. Their hope is to make films and documentaries with their partner in the future. You can find them on Instagram and TikTok.

Isabella Vancartier

I'm Isabella Vancartier from Lawton Oklahoma my given name is Thomas Emanuel Edwards Thurman. I've been a female impersonator for the last 21 years. I've been the promoter for the second oldest preliminary to miss gay Oklahoma America Miss Gay Lawton Oklahoma America for the last 7 years. I'm the current reigning Miss Gay Arkansas USofA 2019, and Miss Gay Oklahoma USofA 2022. I'm also a tailor for the United States Army for the last 10 years, and a civil service employee for the commissary here at fort sill Oklahoma. Photo Credit: Carrie Strong

Jack Diamond

Jack Diamond is an actor, and a DRAG King. He has been doing DRAG since 2015. Jack Diamond is based in Pittsburgh, Pennsylvania, United States. In 2018 he started a DRAG and variety show called Unique! which has raised hundreds of dollars for various nonprofit organizations. The show was designed to be sensory friendly, accessible, and family friendly. When it comes to genres, this King does a variety with his DRAG. It really depends on the theme of the show and what song would fit the theme. He is currently a member of Hot Metal Hardware, and Mr. Pennsylvania Trans Pride 2022.

Jacquelynn Gillian

My name is Jacquelynn Gillian. I'm a southern debutant from Alabama, inspired by the glamour and beauty of films of the 1950's and 1960s, especially Valley of the Dolls. I love to incorporate my old Hollywood obsessions with more modern artists and fashions that inspire me to create something that is truly me. I really try to make everything I do be something that captures my whole heart and love sharing that with the audience the most.

Check out the book
The Official, Original
DRAG Handbook
From DRAG411

Jade Sotomayor

From the iconic original nine queens of RuPaul's DRAG Race #orginalfish #tradeoftheseason #firstsplit #firstsafe #firstrobbed #snakesontheplane Follow me on Instagram: @jadesotomayor. Twitter @sotomayorjade

Jaded Tucker

Jaded Tucker is a 49 yr old rock God from DeLand Florida. This Sagittarius is new to performing and looks forward to rocking a house close to you soon.

Jakk Bloodstone

I'm Jakk Bloodstone, New England's* punk rock priestess. After spending half of my life helping other realize their vision, in 2020 I set that focus onto myself. I'm different in that I'm not a persona or character, what you see is me at my most powerful. Combining witchcraft and a fearless attitude, I'm here to ensure the next wave of DRAG artists knows they don't have to listen to anyone's rules but their own. I spent the first fourteen years of my life learning performance, finding every opportunity out there for a creative kid with no money. The feeling of bringing all of those things to the stage finally, is one I still have trouble describing. A mixture of dance, contortions, flow arts and witchcraft make up my high energy DRAG. You can find me on Instagram at @jakk_bloodstone. I'm available for bookings and love to fly!

* *New England is a northeastern region of the United States comprising the states of New Hampshire, Massachusetts, Maine, Vermont, Connecticut and Rhode Island.*

James "The King" Jackson

James 'The King' Jackson is a punk rock, horror King who loves to get filthy and fabulous, located at New Port Richey, Florida, United States. He might still be a baby King, of nineteen years old, but he'll claw his way and snatch everyone's hearts away. His main goals include being on the hit TV show "Dragula" and snatching the crown, and to spread the message that horror DRAG is beautiful and deserves to be heard. Being a DRAG King makes me feel like I can be myself, and show my twisted, dark side on DRAG. Follow him on Instagram: James.the.king.jackson. Follow him on Facebook: James Jackson.

James Cass

In 2021, I began to hit the stage regularly at the Connection Nightclub of Davenport, Iowa. My journey and passion to make a difference in the world pointed to the pageantry systems. I've roamed the Midwest to Central Florida. I started King Cass Production which made its debut during COVID-19 lock down on YouTube raising money for a hand full of nonprofits and now produces themed events with nationally known entertainers. I hold the title of Trans Masculine representative of Come Out St Pete, a nonprofit organization, to raise money for many different causes. I'm simply unapologetically me and proud of it.

James Gemini Rose

James Gemini Rose is a variety King from South Dakota. As one of the first of two Kings to premier in Rapid City he gained the title of King of the Black Hills. He loves surprising the audience and entertaining all ages. He was adopted into the well-known Rose family and strives to live up to the name given to him. His favorite number so far is a reverse strip tease done to the song "Pants" by Here Come the Mummies.

Jason Beauregard

I do DRAG because I can! I was born in 1955, the same year as rock 'n' roll. According to Mom, that was the problem, but that problem tattooed music to my soul. My teenage years were spent wrapped around a radio, developing an eclectic taste in music, and collecting a massive amount of vinyl. Because of this, I do a great deal of old school retro. I am a gender illusionist, fooling more than one person, passing for male. A double dog dare put me on the stage, and Jason Beauregard just happened. Finally, I had an outlet where I could share my diverse musical knowledge to multiple generations. It also helped me with the lifetime of confusion I had about which one was the opposite sex. DRAG allows me to be unpredictable. Whether I am performing old school rock or something serious or "Rainbow Connection" dressed as a frog, I get to watch the reactions on the faces of the people there as I wander around the stage. Do you know how difficult it is to waltz in flippers? I have to pick my songs very carefully, because I really can't dance. The lyrics, emotion and the reaction of any song I perform is very important to me. Words and music; words and music. What else can I say? *Photo Credit: Kate Jones*

Jelly Cube

Hello! It's me, Jelly Cube! I'm the multi-coloured, eccentric from Abingdon, Oxfordshire, England, United Kingdom. Known for my vocals, love for anything edible and ever-changing style and campery. I use my DRAG as a form of expression and a way of tapping into my inner femininity and helping others with their confidence as well. Within my four-year career, I've hosted events, done live vocal sets, performed in the finale of a lip-sync competition and headlined Pride! You can find me in Oxfordshire and The West Midlands at venues like Glamorous, The White Lion in Tamworth and more! When I'm not the beast Jelly, you'll find me producing original music and remixes for myself and half of the electronic duo The Gliding Faces. Furthermore, I create Digital Art through the Instagram page @Jellypopz. I sew my own outfits, craft jewelry, style wigs and have a whole surfeit of hobbies and talents. My goal in DRAG is to be known across the world and to be sought after for my souring vocals and chaotic disposition, touring the country and perhaps the world! You can find me on Instagram at @jellyqb and on Facebook at the page and profile of Jelly Cube.

Jenna Saisquoix

Jenna Saisquoix takes her name from the French expression, meaning "a quality that cannot be named or described easily." In her mind, the purpose of any art is to work like a wordless language and bring differently minded people together. Her love of theatre, camp, and silliness goes back to age four, when she picked up her first Barbie doll and started creating stories. Now 22, Jenna spends her days pretty similarly, except she now is the Barbie doll. She is an Oregon, United States native, born and raised in Salem, and currently living in Portland. Jenna frequents the stages of popular venues in the area such as The Queen's Head and Darcelle XV. Jenna and her DRAG sister Bleu Dinah host and produce the biggest DRAG show in Southern Oregon, "Bleuprint". Jenna hopes to spend the rest of her life exploring and celebrating the art form she is so passionate about.

Jennifer Foxx

Originally from River Rouge, a suburb of Detroit, Michigan, United States. I recently celebrated 42 years in the art form of female impersonation as a male actress/ celebrity illusionist. Credits include Miss Gay America 1982 and headlining / Master of Ceremonies positions as Mr. Joan Rivers in the productions of " An Evening at La Cage " and "Frank Marino's Divas" Las Vegas, Nevada, Atlantic City, New Jersey, Honolulu, Hawaii, Reno, Nevada, Laughlin, Nevada, and Caesars Windsor, Ontario, Canada. Also honored to hold the distinction of being the first female impersonator to appear ever on nationally syndicated television NBC's The Tom Snyder Tomorrow Show along with my mother. I am still performing regularly and preparing for yet another tour to begin later this year. *Photo Credit: Emin Kuliyev NYNY*

Jerkem All Monroe

Jeri Lee Kitch Also known as Sir Jerkem Monroe began performing in 1986. As a long time Diva performer, Jerkem is my alter ego. He has performed at many clubs but has had the habit of staying close to home. He has been known to be utterly romantic, vampiric, then at the drop of a coin he is a streaking lush! Not bad for a 52-year-old Mother to ten grown kids! Jerkem loves performing at Someplace Else Night Club in Evansville Indiana, United States but willing to darken any door step!

Jerry Diesel

Jerome "Jerry" Diesel from Parts Unknown. The supposed cousin of "Vince Diesel," Jerry is what you get when an immigrant who only grew up watching Albanian soap operas becomes a performer. He is known for ambitious concept and adequate execution. He might be new to the game but he will chew the scenery up. He currently resides in Denver, Colorado, United State. *Photo Credit: Miguel Casino*

Jesse Love

Jesse Love is a charity DRAG King who loves to give back to his community. From Fort Worth, Texas, United States. Jesse Love is the current Imperial Crown Prince of the Imperial Court de' Fort Worth/Arlington; a 501(c) non-profit organization that gives back to LGBTQ+ communities. He started DRAG about three years ago and has always done shows that help raise money for charities. Jesse has always had a passion for theatre and currently works at a haunted house, which inspires some spooky themed numbers at shows. Even though he is new to the DRAG scene, Jesse Love has a huge heart for helping others and one day hopes to make a huge impact for the community.

Check out the book DRAG King Guide From DRAG411

Jimmy Emerson

Jimmy Emerson was born and started his career in Texas, but his talents as an actor and comedian caught the attention of Las Vegas producers, and he moved to Las Vegas where he immediately starting working as a comedy female impersonator on the Strip. Starring in An Evening at La Cage at the Riviera, impersonating stars like Roseanne Barr, Peggy Lee, Anna Nicole Smith, Ann Miller, Cher, Britney Spears, Mama Cass, Judge Judy, Ethel Merman and others, Jimmy not only got rave reviews at the Riviera show, but he also toured nationally and internationally with the road company of La Cage to multiple cities and countries, including Biloxi, San Francisco, Reno, New York, Atlantic City, London, Aruba, with several special appearances in South America. When Jimmy was not working in La Cage he was appearing in the comedy revue show, Bottoms Up. In Bottoms Up Jimmy appeared in and out of DRAG, still delivering fast paced comedy lines and routines. When La Cage closed in 2009, Jimmy went with Frank Marino to his show Divas and appeared in the show as Wynonna Judd, and was Frank's permanent understudy. Photo Credit: James Peterson

Joey Brooks

Joey is a Tampa native and has been in show business ever since he was seventeen years old. He started off his career right here on 7th Avenue in Ybor City, Tampa, Florida, United States at the world famous El Goya. Joey has been working very hard at his craft as the Show Director and MC for El Goya, Tracks, Pleasure Dome and many other clubs in the Tampa Bay area. Joey has toured all over the world from Tampa to Rio, London, Amsterdam and many others. While on Tour, he worked in several world-class shows like Masquerade Follies, La Cage, and the world-famous Finocchio's in San Francisco. Joey was featured as Dolly Parton, Charro, Tammy Fae Baker and many more Illusions in these shows. He also has a book "The Show Must Goes On" and a short movie "Joey's Show Must Go On."

Jonah The Godfather of Drag

Jonah has been performing since 2000. He started his career at Blake's with a few legendary queens of St Louis, Missouri, United States. He went on to direct the Monday Night King Show at Novak's, The FRatPack Show at Rehab, and SWAG at R-Bar. Jonah was the King of Novak's in 2007 and King of Pride STL in 2012. Afterwards, he reunited with his beloved Queen family, The Original Broads of Broadway that still perform at Bar PM. The FRatPack show has also been revived and features his DRAG brothers at Bar PM. Jonah coordinates the Annual Tips for TaTas Breast Cancer Fundraiser, which has been going on for fifteen years, and participates in many other benefits throughout the year. He is also very involved with the Pride STL Royalty Committee. You can see Jonah at various venues around St Louis and in Illinois as well.

Jonlly Reigns St. Martin

Hello! I'm Jonlly Reigns St. Martin! I'm a non-binary DRAG performer who loves doing out of the box DRAG. I enjoy doing anything possible for the community, and even help brought the first ever LGBT safe space to Clayton, GA. My goal is to not only bring change outside of the community, but inside as well. The thought of having more non-binary representation within the DRAG community would be a dream come true. DRAG for me is my pride and joy, to be able to express how I feel through art is all I want in life.

Josie Purée

"A purple haired starlight looking for her chance to shine bright! Only a year into the Denver and Boulder, Colorado DRAG scene. Miss Puree loves to warm the hearts around her and make you feel good while keeping it classy. She loves a good charity event and anything around community engagement. Reminding us all to "Stay Tuned, Get Blended." @josiepuree on all social media.

Julia D'Poon

Julia D'Poon residing in Seattle, Washington United States. I first performed in Louisiana, United States in 1970. I achieved Ms Gay Louisiana in 1974. I have lived/performed in Seattle, Washington United States having now the longest running DRAG/Karaoke in the City. I am followed on Facebook and Instagram and with The Crescent Lounge, Seattle, Washington United States. I am proudly 72 years old. I continue to support and coach the young ones coming in, especially the number of Trans that are entering our arena. My mantras are use your voice and be heard. If you see it, you can do it, so believe in yourself and how do you know you will fail when you don't try.

Check out the book
DRAG Queen Guide
From DRAG411

Jushtin Butterfly

I am Ty Kingsberry and I'm known as Jushtin Butterfly, a voice actor and cosplayer by day and a DRAG King by night. Currently Jushtin is living and performing in Richmond, Virginia, United States. I am the current host of the Butterfly Talent Show and Total Request DRAG both virtual shows on Instagram. You can always catch me at a DRAG show, karaoke, or supporting friends. I love making new outfits and songs for DRAG numbers and I hope to one day share my shows with the world

Justice Twist

Justice Twist is a DRAG King currently residing in Wilkes Barre, Pennsylvania, United States who started performing in late 2019. Best known for his obsession with glitter, stones and leather, over the top costumes, quirky numbers and live vocals. He loves to keep people guessing as to what he will come up with next, consistently blurring the lines between gender norms. He is your 2019/2020 Mr. NEPA PrideFest, Mr. Pottsville Pride 2021, Lebanon Grand Divo 2021, and current Mr. 12 Penny 2022. When not performing he can be found costume designing, photographing and working backstage at local theatres. He also runs a successful all ages, DRAG camp and show and is a huge advocate for sober all ages queer spaces. Outside of DRAG he sits on multiple community committees that strive to make a difference in his surrounding area. Follow him on Instagram @justice_twist and facebook as Justice Twist.

DRAG411.com
7,000 Performers in 32 Countries

Justin Betweener

Justin Betweener was born and raised in New Orleans. Performing in the city since 2008 where he started to blossom both on stage and on the microphone. He has been producing and hosting shows since 2009. A trained dancer; he brings the high energy dance numbers with a side of stripping. A comedian in his own way, hoping to bring the joy of DRAG to anyone open to experience it. He hopes to build up the King/Diva DRAG scene in the city and offer opportunities to those starting out. Mr. New Orleans Pride 2020. Mr. Louisiana USofA MI first alternate 2022. For bookings: justinbetweenerDRAG@gmail.com.

Justin Case

Justin Case is the current reigning Mister USofA Classic MI and also Arkansas, United States' reigning Mister USofA Classic MI. He is the oldest performer to ever hold the national title. He has been performing for over fifteen years in various venues and carries many titles. However, what he wants most for other performers to know is to always follow your heart and to always pay it forward. There are way too many folks he can thank for all of the life gifts he has received, so paying it forward to those who need a helping hand is his life goal.

Check out the book
Winning Pageants
By DRAG411

Justin Sane

Hello there, I am Justin Sane, pronounced Just-in-sane. I am a non-binary King who found their way into DRAG on July 4, 2020 in Columbus, Georgia, United States. The very next time I hopped on the stage I won the title of Mr. Columbus Pride of 2020. During my reign I started a nonprofit named "Just Me" based around education, validation, and resources to help our youth and their families/friends who support. I know both sides of being an LGBTQ+ youth as well as the worries parents have since I'm a bio mother to three kiddos. I moved to Denver Colorado in September of 2021 and right working on running for the MX title during The Gay Pride of Colorado pageant. "To truly love yourself, you must be yourself completely."

Justin Syde

He razzles. He dazzles. It's Justin Syde! This Immaculate Conception has been lip-syncing for longer than he will ever admit, and donned a beard in more dives than any millennial club kid could ever remember. A Romanichal descendant, with deep Albertan roots, Justin (aka Marissa) resides in Calgary, Canada with her wife – queerlesque dancer Imogen Rouge (Siobhán.) Having lived in both Canada and France, they've been a passionate advocate, met countless amazing folks, and involved with many Community groups. Educating with AIDS Vancouver Island's OutSpeak team, demonstrating in the Rhône-Alpes, serving as Camosun College's Pride Director, joining Calgary Outlink's board, and hosting Okotoks' first Pride are some highlights from their gay-sumé. In DRAG, Justin was crowned Mr. Gay Vancouver Island 2010, informally known as the "femmest Mr. Gay ever." He was also appointed the 35th Count of the Imperial Sovereign Court of the Chinook Arch. With that dragon eye twinkle and some tricks up his sleeve, this DRAG King extraordinaire always has a tale to tell &

guarantees you won't forget his swooney style or glitzy garb anytime soon, regardless of where you happen upon him. Connect at @MrJustinSyde or check out linktr.ee/MisbegottenHobbies. Photo Credit: Burlesque Burn Flirtfest10, Darryl Boehm/Slider Photography"

Justin Tyme

Justin Tyme is a Houston, Texas, United States based DRAG King. They have been performing for seven years. They got their start with Houston Gaymers and was doing DRAG as a hobby. Now they perform live at Pearl bar Houston. They are known for their comic book stylized makeup. They are the Rock King of Houston, Texas, United States. They also perform and participate in digital competitions. Winning their first competition Camp Kamikaze season 3 and aiming to win dragging faerie tales. They love Rock and roll, fantasy and leather. You can find them on Instagram @justintymedrag

Kade Jackwell

I began my DRAG performance career in 2016 after many years of costuming and cosplay work. Performing on a DRAG stage is a completely different experience than a cosplay stage, and I've enjoyed becoming a part of the DRAG community. In 2019, I ran for and won the title of MsTer MGRA (Missouri Gay Rodeo Association) and in 2020 I entered the international level of the same competition. I held the title of MsTer IGRA for 2020-2021. Currently I am best known as the "Rhinestone Cowboy" of Kansas City, Missouri, United Sttes and travel to perform all around the Midwest.

Kade Lovewell

My name is Kade Lovewell but y'all can call me daddy. I am diverse, fun loving, and like to have a good time. I am always down to helping the community and fellow DRAG entertainers. I've been doing DRAG for thirteen years now. I am a former Mr. Garden 2012 and I am current Mr. LOIA (Lesbians of Iowa, United States) titleholder. I am also a part of two amazing groups, The DSM Kings and the Kapital City Kings; so, you can say Kade Lovewell is the King of the community.

Kahtya Tehnsion

I'm Kahtya Tehnsion, mother of the Iconic Haus of Tehnsion, 27 years old from Fort Lauderdale, Florida, United States. I've been entertaining for six years, where I've headlined, performed, and hosted across the country. You can describe my DRAG as "timeless with a little spice". I mostly do comedy, but I thoroughly enjoy high glamor DRAG. I've won many titles, produced and emceed many successful shows, and I style wigs for Queens across the country.

Kai

Kai is a 27-year-old baby DRAG King who recently started performing at the beginning of 2022. He is the current resident DRAG King at Splash Bar in Modesto, California, United States; he frequents The Brave Bull in Modesto as well. Kai, like a true Gemini, is a double-edged sword on the stage. His routines can vary greatly from a goofy comedian, to a dapper gentleman, to a dominant daddy. His wardrobe choices also reflect his chameleon-like personality. Kai is known to wear quirky costumes, sophisticated suits, as well as leather and chest harnesses. He is goofy, laid-back, and cares deeply about his fellow DRAG artists and neighborhood queer community. Kai knows how to show the crowd a good time; he is well known for actively interacting with audience members-especially during his "spicier" dance routines. Although he is just starting out, Kai has gained some noticeable recognition at his local DRAG scene. He hopes to start performing all over the state of California and eventually across the county. Kai is active on the social media platforms of Instagram, Twitter, and TikTok @kaithedragking and is available for booking opportunities by messaging any of the above-mentioned accounts. Photo Credit: Jaime Heilman

Kai Kade

I started this year. I'm 36 and I loved DRAG since I was about 20 years old. I love to perform and I love making people smile and laugh at the same time. I'm from Texas but I do love to travel and love to drive. I go by Taylor and stage name Kai Kade. I choose the name because it's rare and different. I picked Kai as my middle as my legal name too. I love kids and meeting new people. I love learning new songs and learning anything new to be honest. I'm a fast learner. Kai is a funny guy and flirts and a goof ball. Plus, I've been told he is a handsome boy band male. Kai loves suits and the vests.

Kale Green the Drag King

Kale Green the DRAG King is the DRAG equivalent of a Spirit Halloween that used to be a Whole Foods. He started his DRAG career in Ithaca, New York, United States during the summer of 2017. Now residing in Charlotte, North Carolina, he has performed in shows all over New York state, the Carolinas, and the Internet via virtual shows. In May of 2021, he was crowned "Most Angsty" at the Flamies,

Who's Who of DRAG

hosted by Flame Night Fever. When he's not bathing in glitter and fake blood at DRAG shows, Kale can be found working as a haunt actor, spending time cosplaying, or playing with his cat, Matcha, who he claims is his soulmate and muse.

Karl Withakay

Karl Withakay is a newer DRAG King from Deland, Florida, United States. He enjoys performing for the community, making people laugh (and a little uncomfortable), and long walks on the beach. Known for his purple mohawk, swagger, interesting choices of music, and double entendres, he is your inner voice, personified. Karl plans to compete for the next Mr. Deland Pride title at the Deland Pride Pageant in January 2023. He is suave, sexy, and sophisticated. He is the most interesting man in Deland. Keep an eye out for Karl Withakay, because he is an up-and-comer! You can follow him on Facebook at KarlWithakay.DragKing.

Karmella Uchawi

Karmella Uchawi is the Bearded Banjee of Kansas City, Missouri, United States! She is a bearded beauty who loves to bring life to the party. Whether that be twerking to the latest bop or serving mug in the brightest of outfits. She loves to dance, loves to get the crowd hyped, and loves to give positive energy. She's always going to make sure it has little Black Girl Mella Magic twist. She got her start in the open show scene in Kansas City. After repeatedly showing up and showing out, she has quickly grown to be a main performer in her city. Now, after four years of performing, she is continuously trying to reach new heights and perform all over. Performing is what brings her the most joy and happiness because entertaining is what she loves. You can keep up with her on Instagram, Tiktok, and Twitter @thekarmella and @Karmella Uchawi on Facebook. Photo Credit: Zanny Ex

Katrina Victim

Hello, my name is Katrina Victim. I am originally from New Orleans, Louisiana, United States and currently reside in Lexington, Kentucky. I started doing DRAG over three years ago and continued paving my own path in DRAG since. I currently host an open stage here in the area that all types of DRAG are welcomed. Between dropping levees on a stage near you to cooking is my passion. I would describe my DRAG fun, campy, someone who just likes to have a good ol' time. I do love standing out and being different. I started with bearded DRAG and every once in a while, we will go from tuna casserole to big mouth bass when I shave my beard, just to mix it up. Hope to be in a town near you soon! For booking or inquires feel free to message me on Facebook or just give my Facebook page a message at Katrina Victim Peace, love, and ham hock grease!

KayKay Lavelle

KayKay Lavelle is the South East United States' premiere bearded queen! From New York City to Miami, and into international waters, KayKay has graced the stages of many, being the cornerstone of old school and new school DRAG. KayKay has been featured on the cover of queer magazines such as QNotes and YesWeekly! as well as being covered in NewNowNext and Queerty for her trailblazing efforts. KayKay has hosted bear events and even performed on bear cruises to international level. KayKay was also featured in Season 2 of Hightown on Starz. Breaking the glass ceiling of the pageant world by being the first bearded Queen to qualify and compete at National Entertainer of the Year in 2018, KayKay strives to show the world that there's nothing wrong with being big, bold and beautiful. Find her on Instagram @kaykaylavelle

Who's Who of DRAG

KC StarrZ

KC StarrZ relocated to Tampa, Florida from sunny San Diego with her husband Denny in June 2021. She is a talented entertainer and former cast member of two long standing shows in San Diego's Hillcrest neighborhood, Dollhouse and Vanity Hour, and also left behind her own show, Jam Session, and her spot as a resident Queen and Show Hostess at #1 Fifth Avenue in San Diego. She also enjoys singing, and in 2010 was the first person crowned Arizona Country Idol. She was the creator, owner and past producer of the California Regional Bearded Queen pageant, past Abbess of the San Diego Sisters of Perpetual Indulgence and current promoter for the National Southeast Bearded Queen Pageant. She also designs and creates custom clothing and gowns for herself and others with clients in the US, Canada, and Europe. She now holds the title of National Bearded Empress Emeritus de Gentillesse and is an ambassador for Non-Binary Bearded Performers.

Keisha Kye

My name is Keisha Kye and I live in Tulsa, Oklahoma, United States. I'm a 32-year veteran to DRAG and am 49 years old. I've won many titles throughout the years from bar to national. I am involved in community growth through the local Equality Center and Grateful Day Foundation. While I've enjoyed many aspects of the art, I'm most happy hosting my shows, being on the mic and making people laugh. Someday, I think I'll try my hand at stand up, but otherwise, I'm very content with my accomplishments to date. Contact me through Facebook or email: missvintageans2015@gmail.com for more. *Photo Credit: Melissa Mooney Photography*

Kelly Powers

Oklahoma City, Oklahoma, United States. 44 years young! I am from the great state of Oklahoma. I've been performing DRAG and practicing the art of female impersonation for 23 years. I've performed in many clubs, parades, venues, and backseats all over the US and twice in Europe. I love to bring an audience to the edge with my filthy yet respectful mouth, while on the microphone. I can give everyone a true memorable entertainment experience. In my personal life, I work in dentistry, have four children, and one grand baby. Hope to see y'all in the dressing rooms!

Kenneth J. Squires

Kenneth J. Squires is a 56-year-old DRAG King. Originally from California, United States is now living in Kentucky. Kenneth is a member of The Imperial Court of Kentucky, Kentucky Bourbon Bears, and does shows for charity events. Kenneth has won King of DRAG 2013, Mister Gay Valentine 2014, 2nd place in JR's Unlimited Contest and Mr. Mary Christmas 2019. He has also won from the ICK the "Falsie" award three times for outstanding achievement in male impersonation. Kenneth still does DRAG, and is excited to be performing in the first Mt. Sterling's first Pride event.

Check out the book
DRAG Mother, DRAG Father
Honoring Your Mentors
From DRAG411

Kilda Mann

Kilda Mann is a non-binary DRAG Queen from Des Moines, Iowa, United States. They mostly do alternative DRAG; however, they're known for being versatile and dipping into several types of DRAG. They love to do ballet and their performances in their pointe shoes always have the crowd drawn in. Kilda is also a huge advocate for representation of people of all genders in the DRAG scene. They want to use their platform to bring light and work to eliminate transphobia and misogyny present in the DRAG world.

Killa Watt

Killa Watt's performances and personas are neither created nor destroyed. Their performances are a constant source of transformation and evolution. These performances are a blend of rock, nerd, geek and everything in between. Let Killa Watt resonate in your neuro-circuits. Killa Watt was born as a DRAG King at Didi's Playhaus 2017 in Lethbridge, Alberta, Canada on Treaty 7 Territory, Traditional lands of the Blackfoot and Métis. Their parents are David McFall and DRAG Mothers Aria Ivory and Sophie Wright (Thanks and luv to you!) In 2018 they transitioned to a DRAG Monarch. As of 2020 they reside in Saskatoon, Saskatchewan, Canada on Treaty 6 Territory, Traditional lands of the Cree and Homeland of the Métis. The goal of their DRAG is to mesh the fabulousness of DRAG with Science and use the platforms provided to them to explore science and society and help move our world in dealing with Climate Change and other systemic issues. Instagram @killawatt.hausdidi. YouTube: Killa Watt. Twitter @KillaWatt_HD. Facebook: Killa Watt. Tik Tok @dolphinashamrock

King Blaze Khrystian

Onstage, I am known as King Blaze Khrystian. I began my journey to become a DRAG King over fourteen years ago, all because I was told I would never "make it" as a performer. I am honored to say that after holding two crowns and four sashes for titles that I never dreamed I could achieve; I am still perfecting my craft. I am known by my iconic Mohawk and my love of rock. Keep dreaming and never let anyone tell you what your worth is. I have been the King of Tulsa Pride as well as a state and city titleholder. Believe in yourself and never let your dreams go. *Photo Credit: Carrie Strong*

King Crimson

666-year-old, vampire, warrior and devilish DRAG King, residing in the United Kingdom. A master of ceremonies, international cabaret artist and lover of all things theatrical, dramatic, camp and cinematic. This King started their DRAG journey during the lockdown of 2021 and has been performing regularly ever since. Appearing live at Cabaret, DRAG and Burlesque shows, virtual online and other events across the United Kingdom and beyond. Big DRAG Pageant UK - Finalist 2022. Host - The Leeds Tattoo Exposition, UK. 2022. Featured King in the International DRAG Book- DRAG 411. Member of The Scarlet Vixens, UK. Member of Hastings Queer Collective, UK. Equity member. Fire Performer. Socials. Facebook @kingcrimsonDRAG. Instagram @king_crimson666. *Photo Credit. Barry Yellow.*

King Mykal Khrystian

King Mykal Khrystian started out as one of the first DRAG Kings in the Tulsa, Oklahoma, United States area over twenty years ago. He started his humble beginnings performing with local DRAG queens, whom he learned most of his techniques from. Over time he watched the DRAG King community grow around him into what it is today. He has held multiple titles, including the first Oklahoma M.I. title, Mr. Gay Oklahoma USA FMI 2006. After a break from the stage, he returned in 2016 winning Mister Oklahoma USofA M.I. Classic, and again in 2017 winning Mister Route 66 USofA M.I. Classic. In the last year he has proudly held the title of King of Tulsa Pride 2022, and made himself a home at a local bar, CLJs. He truly loves what he does and despite his age doesn't see stopping anytime soon. In fact, he's just getting started. *Photo credit: Eden Grace Wilde*

King Nilus

My name is King Nilus and I am a DRAG performer based in Upstate New York, United States. I have been doing DRAG for three years and have used my love for rock as my muse for my performances. So far, I've performed mainly in New York and New Jersey but my big goals are to perform on stage worldwide. Although I may be a relatively young King and new to the scene, I want to use my background in the arts to make the sky the limit for my passion for my DRAG. I'm constantly exploring new shapes and sizes when it comes to facial hair, wigs and costumes. Performing has been a desire of mine since I was young but I wasn't sure of a uniqueness to call my own. I did masquerade dance performances at cosplay events but I knew there was something more I wanted to explore besides cross play. DRAG opened my eyes to limitless new ways of self-expression. I aspire to be my own character, to be in the lights, with the music loud, and my everything on fleek. With DRAG in my life, my creative outlets are better fulfilled on stage.

King Perka $exxx

King Perka $exxx is an Atlanta, Georgia, United States made but Charlotte, North Carolina based DRAG King who brings you comedy, social commentary and dad jokes. He is based in the Southeast of the United States and is known for his travels bringing his unique take on this art to many corners of the country.

King Vaughnz Spanic

King Vaughnz Spanic is a charming and talented Latinx heartthrob, starting in Boulder, Colorado, United States (now between there and Irvine, California), taking on different cities and states at a time. He is a non-binary trans masculine King, representing the Haus of Spanic and is one of Colorado's Freshest Faces 2022. They give you high energy performances, but also knows how to touch your heart, ranging from selling sex to vulnerability in sharing his story. King started DRAG in 2019 at his school's annual DRAG show as a freshman at the age of 18. As soon as he started, they built a reputation for professionalism and was allowed to perform in 21+ venues, even competing and placing nineth out of nineteen in his first pageant as Mister Gay Colorado United States MI 2020 in Roanoke, VA. To prove his commitment, he would bus hours for an unpaid show, leading him to where he's at. Unfortunately, his journey started with disapproval from family, but he has been able to rekindle relationships and show, and others, the importance of DRAG. Through his DRAG, King hopes to inspire others with their journey with representation. Instagram @kingvaughnzspanic. *Picture Credit: Gage Stirsman*

Who's Who of DRAG

King Vyper

King Vyper is South Florida's Slithery and Sinister Ghoul. Vyper's DRAG is what you get when you cross the Matrix, Blade, and a bit of cosplay. Leather, harnesses, spikes, studs, and chains are just a few things you'd see him bring to the stage, along with some sexy dance moves, conceptual storytelling, and captivating performances! Vyper is always available to collaborate with other queer artists, photographers, and other entertainers, as well as travel for shows & bookings. He's even traveled to places like Denver, Colorado, Houston, Texas and even New York City (all in the United States). King Vyper aspires to be a household name for the King community, representing AMAB* DRAG Kings across the globe. And who knows? Maybe we might get to see him on Dragula one day... Follow King Vyper on Instagram, TikTok, and Twitter at @kingvyper66 *Photo Credit: Lazaro Ricardo*
* *Assigned male at birth*

King-Sparkles Royale-Capri

Orlando's Newest live singing DRAG King. I'm a fashion King that's not scared to show a little body and even do tricks and kicks

These performers come from around the world. Thank you for learning about DRAG In other Nations!

Kitty Quinn Khrystian

Kitty Quinn Khrystian is a Tulsa, Oklahoma, United States based performer performing in a circus sideshow and belly dancer, getting invited to guest perform in the local DRAG scene before she began her DRAG career over ten years ago. Her performance style ranges in many categories but is notoriously known for her ease into Broadway performances and loves doing characters. She later evolved her career more by participating in pageants and recently snagged the crown as Queen of Tulsa Pride 2022. Kitty is always evolving. She can also be found in her other alter ego as King TomCat Khrystian making this entertainer quite versatile. Instagram: kitty_the_dark. Facebook: Dayna E.VanHauen

Konstance Panic

My stage name reflects my normal physical state, which is completely riddled with anxiety. However, in DRAG, I don't feel that "Panic." I feel confident; whole. I used to think of DRAG as a mask that I could throw on, become someone else for a little while and be that confident, rambunctious person. I was wrong, Konstance wasn't a mask, but she was an extension of me. She's who I am when my brain doesn't default to panic mode. She's me, just with a lot more makeup and a lot more sequins.

It's time to check out
DRAG411.com

Kraven Moorehead

Hello, Fellas! I'm Kraven Moorehead. And if you are too, let's discuss it. This mouth does a lot. I am a glamour clown and a dad body in a dress. If you want to order a burger, just tell loudly into this clown's mouth. I am from St. Petersburg, Florida, United States but currently living in Chicago. I'm a Cub's fan. If it's funny, I'm there!

Kruz Mhee

Hello from Birmingham, Alabama, United States. My name is Kruz Mhee "The God Father". More recently known as Kruz Mhee Davidson. I have been performing in the state of Alabama, United States and other outlying southern states since 1994. In the early 90s I was known as Paula, which is my real name and I performed what was called Faux DRAG but now called bio queen. In 2007 I transitioned fully to male impersonation, also known as DRAG King. I've won titles competing in both styles of DRAG: Ms. Bills Club 1994, Mister Central Alabama Pride 2007, Quest Club King, Mr. Platinum Icon, emeritus and most recently Mr. Alabama USA Unlimited 2022. In my time as a male impersonator, I've had the pleasure of founding and running three amazing performance crews. Generation NxXxT was my All-Female cast that performed together for five years, which made us the longest running all female show in a "Home bar" in Alabama. Then the Magic City K!NGz and Dollz and finally The Magic City Marvels. Now I spend most of my DRAG time working with local nonprofit organizations to help raise funds for those in need. DRAG has been the best creative outlet for me. I've met so many people, fans and friends. Thanks, in a way, to DRAG for meeting my beautiful wife. It's been a 28-year ride in the DRAG community. I can't wait to see what's next.

Krymson Scholar

This is how I ended up on the many stages as Krymson Scholar. My husband introduced me to the DRAG world and I fell in love. I would perform for him all the time in the beginning. He would tell me I belong on stage. I started performing at local DRAG clubs in Mississippi and Alabama, United States and loved it. I love seeing the smiles on people's faces and the joy they have singing along to the songs I performed. After performing for several years all over the south my husband and I decided to pack up our lives in Mississippi and move to New York City. I eventually joined LadyQueen Collective, a group of cis, AFAB, non-binary trans identified performing collective based in Brooklyn, New York I also became part of The Nobodies also based in Brooklyn and after 2 years of living there I then moved to Philadelphia, Pennsylvania and started doing many shows here and there still to this day.

Krystal Cain

"I was born with a twin sister; we are best friends, but I view Krystal as what my sister would have had if I was born a girl. I've been performing for ten years now, I live in Sandusky, Ohio and one of the house Queens at Sandusky Crowbar. DRAG for her, is over the top. Big hair, big jewelry, big personality. She loves the 90's, especially the power divas of country." Photo Credit: Sandusky Crowbar Staff

DRAG411.com
Documenting the DRAG Community
Since 2010 in Print

Lady Cynthia

Lady Cynthia, 58 years young. I started my career as a female impersonator in the early 1990s in Chicago and performed at various clubs including the Baton Show Lounge I competed in several pageants throughout my career and have traveled all over the United States. My titles include Miss Club Med in Louisiana, Miss Gigi's Classic in Michigan, and Miss Purple Angle Continental Elite, where I placed top 10 in Chicago at nationals. I have been Miss Rainbow Room Classic in Michigan and Miss Glass Citi Classic in Ohio I have met several celebrities and made many friends along the way. I'm old school and a well-seasoned performer. I have judged many pageants and gave advice to many girls.I still to this day get nervous when I hit the stage

Lady Laquelle

Lady Laquelle is originally from Sturbridge, Massachusetts, United States but didn't come out of the casket until she moved to Sarasota, Florida. Eschewing the standard DRAG model of giant blond wigs, lip syncing and death drops, she prefers to sing in her own natural bass-baritone and writes her own song parodies. Homemade videos for her parodies can be seen on YouTube among her other creative works, while the songs themselves can be heard on SoundCloud. Since 2017, Her Ladyship has appeared in venues throughout Sarasota such as the Purple Rhino Lodge and McCurdy's Comedy Club, and performed with such names as Beneva Fruitville and the Black Diamond Burlesque, achieving in that time all the prestige of a sasquatch; seen only in brief glimpses and remembered only in vague stirrings. Her day will come though. *Photo Credit: Goddess Imagery*

Ladycat De'Ore

The Mocha Performance Goddess with 21 years of DRAG. Originally from Brooklyn, New York. Lived and began DRAG in Texas. I now live and perform in Denver, Colorado. I would like to tell you all the stuff I've done and all the places I have been, but that would be too long. I appreciate all forms of DRAG and never stopped trying to grow and learn new thing. Ladycat is a sexy, slutty Goddess. I'm AFAB that also performs female DRAG once a year, I'm a DRAG King and I love my life in DRAG. I'm a DRAG mom of nine DRAG kids, two outlaws, and five grand babies. One day, I might retire, but today is not the day.

Lakeisha Pryce

My name is Walter, better known as Lakeisha Pryce. I've been a DRAG entertainer for 22 years. Over the years I've worked with some of the best entertainers in Athens and Atlanta, Georgia, United States and soon St. Petersburg, Florida. Being a show director, DRAG performer and show host has been some of the most special moments in my DRAG career thus far. Although I may not perform as often as I use to, I still support and give thanks for the ones who helped pave the way for me to become the "Kelly Price" impersonator I am today! Looking forward to entertaining more! Love and lashes, Lakeisha "Big Mama" Pryce.

It's time to check out
DRAG411.com

Leo

Leo the "male feminist" is an Aotearoa, New Zealand based DRAG persona created by performance artist Vixen Temple. Taking influence from '90's grunge/goth, and Temple's ex boyfriends: Leo is a tragic misunderstood artist and aspiring rock star performing in a solo band called "Generic White Male." Leo likes to think of himself as a ladies' man, and is always down to mansplain feminism to the women he's trying to impress. With a Leo sun, Pisces Moon and Scorpio Rising, there's a lot more to Leo than his dashing good looks and arrogance, he is also a sensitive poet who just wants to find somebody to love ... if only he could overcome his toxic masculinity and commitment issues! Perhaps one day he'll settle down, but for now he's living the rock star life and loving every second of it. Photo Credit: Aden Meser

Lily Adonis Fables

22, College Station, Texas, USA. Lily has been doing DRAG for 3 years. During this time, she's been able to make a name for herself as the Season 4 winner of Halo in Bryan, Texas's DRAG-U. She's also competed in Texas A&M University's Draggieland competition. She's also performed in Oklahoma and Arkansas. Her style of performing is generally very pageant and pretty, however she can pull out tricks when needed. She is all for charity work and has worked with local groups sponsoring kitten rescues and children. Her DRAG mom taught her a few universal truths, be who you are, be pretty, and show the world you mean business. As a trans DRAG entertainer, she hopes to inspire future generations of queer youth to be themselves. You can follow her at TheLilyFables on Instagram!

Lily DeVine

Lily Devine is the owner/founder of Showgirls Entertainment and Canadian National Showgirl Pageant (CNSP), she has worked with and volunteered for national charities such as PFLAG Canada, Canadian Mental Health Association (Kingston), and numerous other local charities and organizations. Lily holds the longest running independent show/company in southeastern Ontario for the last ten years, Showgirls Entertainment; while teaching her son that in a world full of hate, be kind. As a previous CNSP Showgirl-at-large 2018 (community appointed), she's a currently reigning Miss Trillium 2021/22 for The Imperial Court of Toronto. Booking: showgirlsentertainmentofficial@gmail.com. She's ready to take on the world, one country at a time! *Photo credit: Nicholas Bryant, 13yrs old, Lily's son*

London DuMore

London DuMore got her start twelve years ago in the small town of Jackson, Mississippi, United States. She started out just performing as a spotlight performer in between numbers. She then started performing regularly all over the states of Mississippi, Louisiana, Alabama, and Tennessee. She did that for about ten years. Recently within the last two years she has semi-retired from the public view and moved to an island in the middle of the west Pacific Ocean. London now calls the island of Saipan in The Commonwealth of Northern Mariana Islands, United States, home. You can catch her most days cutting hair and managing the salon Salt and Barber as her alter ego Curt. Instagram: londondumore. Instagram: hair.by.curt

Who's Who of DRAG

Lord Severus

Lord Severus is the dildo slinging, disabled, DRAG daddy from down under; a professional sex nerd and fetish cabaret queer haunting the gay and metal bars of Meanjin (Brisbane) Australia. A vaudevillian of endless variety, they're a producer, emcee, singer, comedian, burlesquer, parodist, punk poet and codpiece enthusiast. Sev regularly rocks his mobility aids on stage and is deeply committed to disability advocacy and visibility in the arts and LGBTQIA+ community. He's proud to champion body neutrality, fat liberation, trans excellence and disability representation through his style of sex positive, kink charged, low brow yet sincere as hell tomfoolery. He has been honoured with some kickass titles and prizes over the years, including Brisbane Trans Pride Fair Day Pageant winner, DRAG Royale Mr Congeniality, Wham Bam Cabaret Slam winner and Fringe Bar Cabaret Competition Audience Favourite. @DRAGlordsev *Photo Credit: Joel Devereux*

LouAnn Behold

LouAnn Behold is a DRAG Queen out of Vero Beach, FL in the United States of America. Making her public debut in February of 2022, LouAnn can be found cohosting Queerdos and Weirdos; house party themed shows, open stage nights, Sad and Boojie Sundays and karaoke in her hometown. LouAnn was created after getting the life changing experience of playing Pythio in Head Over Heels the musical. All DRAG is valid. DRAG is art. Art is life.

Luke McAnally-Gore-Shadow

Luke McAnally-Gore-Shadow started performing DRAG in 2018; although he had been helping out behind the scenes for a couple years prior to his stage debut. He is a member of the House of Gore and in addition to performing, he works with his DRAG family to organize and promote DRAG shows. He resides in Sault Ste. Marie, Ontario, Canada. Luke's DRAG house is international and he frequently performs in Sault Ste. Marie, Ontario as well as in the twin city in Michigan, United States. He won the DRAG Me to Hell Halloween pageant in 2019 and has held that title for the last few years thanks to COVID preventing competition in 2020 and 2021. While he is locally known as the country King, he enjoys performing to a variety of genres including pop, rock, hip hop, and country. Luke credits DRAG with completely changing his life. Since starting DRAG his daily persona has truly found themselves and the confidence to bust down the closet door and live their most authentic life. You can find Luke on Facebook or Instagram under Luke McAnally-Gore-Shadow.

Luscious L. Minj

Luscious L. Minj is from Detroit, Michigan, United States, and has been described as "A DRAG Queen's DRAG Queen" she loves bringing the classics to the younger age of queens! Luscious was originally created to bring awareness to local nonprofit groups such as FREE MOM HUGS and Affirmations and continues to do so. While not working with nonprofits she's working at Gigi's Gay Bar as the youngest host in the history of the bar! You can find information on WERQ WEDNESDAYS and other shows I take part in on my social media. Facebook: Luscious L. Minj Everything else: @Luscious.Minj.Official

Luz Lips

My name is Luz Lips, and yes, I sink ships. I've got class, I've got sass, and I've got a whole lotta ass. I have been doing DRAG since February 2021, so I'm still fairly new to the scene. But I do DRAG because it empowers me to explore myself, express who I am, and encourage others to do the same. I was born and raised in the Bay Area, and I love being able to give back to my community by working with the Grand Ducal Council of San Francisco, California, United States. I am the current, reigning Miss Debutante, and have helped raise funds for organizations such as the Castro Country Club, Larkin Street Youth Services, and the Transgender Pilot Program. I love being able to make people smile. From dressing up like the Titanic for Celine Dion's "My Heart Will Go On" to mixing Madonna's "Like a Virgin" with Kim Petras' "Treat Me Like a Slut" and "Throat Goat", all who come to see me perform all can agree on one thing: "Luz Lips has loose lips." You can follow the doll on Instagram at @Luz.Lips. You can also follow the dude behind the doll at @TheLuiChavez. *Photo Credit: Kevin Leong*

Mario Wanna

Mario Wanna (He/They) is an androgynous DRAG King based in Colorado Springs, Colorado, United States. Mario started DRAG in 2021 at the age of thirty proving to themself that it is never too late to pursue something that brings you joy. DRAG has really helped give a therapeutic space for artistic expression and has helped heal the way they see their body. This King enjoys portraying anything from the stereotypical fuckboi to conceptual interpretations as well as shining light on social and emotional issues that matter to them through performance. Growing up very involved in theatre and music; he is happy to have found something that incorporates costuming, performance, dancing and occasionally live vocals. They are excited

Who's Who of DRAG

to continue to change the view of what DRAG is in hopes that one day people will see that, just like any other art form, DRAG is subjective and everyone's DRAG is valid. The people who understand will get you while those who don't, aren't for you. "When they go low, he gets high!". Mario hopes to inspire those around him to feel free to be their most authentic and unapologetically unique selves. Facebook: MarioWanna DragKing. Instagram: themariowanna. Booking: mariowannaDRAG@gmail.com.

Maya Shayne

I'm Maya Shayne, aka Barbie Dayne. I have been doing DRAG for thirty plus years. I have worked with many titleholders around the world. I now live in the Clearwater, Florida, United States. I started DRAG in 1992 at Track's El Goya in Ybor City in Tampa, Florida and branched off from there to other bars in other states. I have always been called the Body Beautiful.

Mia Inez Adams

Mature black woman of trans experience. Father. DRAG mother. Entertainer for four decades. Emcee. Promoter of Supernova USofA Newcomer. Girlfriend. Girlfriend. Lover. Fighter. Survivor (eight years cancer free). Cook. Comedienne. Sister. Community activist. All these things and more rolled up into one big friendly bundle of love. *Photo Credit: Scotty Kirby*

DRAG411.com
7,000 Performers in 32 Countries

Michael Monroe

Hi my name is Michael Monroe. I have been a Marilyn Monroe illusionist for fifty years. Divine, the one and only, mentored me for the Miss Baltimore Pageant and I won it in 1973. I am still very active. I am going on a national tour with Jay Miah from The Voice and Alter Egos (on Fox) and The Miah and Monroe Experience. I have always been passionate and met so many amazing people through my long illustrious career! *Photo Credit: Lathala Creative Studio*

Mike Hawk

Mike Hawk is a Portsmouth, New Hampshire, United States based DRAG King who has brought masculine comedy and camp to stages across New England since 2018. A firm believer in the gender neutrality of glitter, Mike combines flamboyant flashy looks with wholesome absurdity and positive masculinity. His performances draw on his experience as a storyteller and his love of comedic irony. Though humor is core to his art, he's known to get serious as well, with deeper explorations of gender, identity, and emotion on stage. Mike's passion for DRAG comes from his local community. Through DRAG, he has discovered found family and he worked to support and build up his community whenever possible, and especially to increase acceptance of DRAG Kings and of all DRAG artists who are assigned female at birth. In 2019, he produced and hosted New Hampshire's first ever all-king DRAG show, and he has continued as a producer to create new queer spaces in New Hampshire and Maine. He has also worked with New England Pride organizations to educate and inspire transgender and gender nonconforming youth. You can find him on Instagram @lovemikehawk.

Miles N. Sider

Hi, I am Miles N. Sider I am a relatively new DRAG King from Marion Ohio, United States. I began doing DRAG in November of 2021. I aspire to inspire positivity through my craft. I travel mostly in northern Ohio; however, I am open to traveling more. I find DRAG to be a creative outlet somewhere to let go and just have fun. I have met some truly incredible people along the way. In the future I plan to not only expand my brand but to compete for titles and become a known name in the industry. it took me several years to find the courage to put myself out there and now that I have it's changed my life for the better. I not only want to be a known name but to be an inspiration for the next generation of entertainers. I am also on Instagram @miles_n_sider. *Photo Credits: Katie Marie*

Mira Shatters

Mira Shatters bloomed late in life as a Queen at 33 years old, starting the journey at 31, but has established her presence in Charleston, South Carolina, United States in less than a year as "The Stomping Queen", a moniker given to her by South Carolina legend Brooke Collins, and is currently an entertainment director at the venue Tin Roof which she co-hosts and runs with her sister Shesha Manson. Blending styles of old-school DRAG with a gothic/punk rock sensibility, she does DRAG on her own terms but strives for growth, always ready to learn from her peers. After playing music for over fifteen years beforehand, Mira grew tired of working with artists that lacked a unified vision. She is finally who she was always meant to be and ready to shatter the world with her absolute dedication to the DRAG artform. *Photo Credit: Shesha Manson*

Mischa Michaels

"The mouth of the north of the Lake" Mischa Michaels is a DRAG Queen who is native to Northeastern Ohio, United States and has been doing DRAG for almost five years. Beginning at All Axs in Willoughby, Ohio. She has been through many challenges but has risen above all of the odds stacked against her! She is now the yearly host of Crawford County Pennsylvania Pride yearly, as well as the host of the online show Makeup with Mischa Michaels. She has performed both physically and digitally all across Ohio, as well as Pennsylvania and West Virginia! You can follow her on Facebook: at Mischa Michaels. Instagram: @Mischamichaels223. YouTube page: Mischamichaels. Tiktok: Mischaandchermichaels.

Miss Conception

With a career spanning over 23 years, Kevin Levesque as Miss Conception, has been delighting audiences around the world with his unique style of female illusion, "a Female Delusionist® if you will", as Kevin puts it. From her beginnings in Toronto, Canada's bar scene, to sell out audiences wherever she appears around the world, Miss Conception has audiences howling with laughter and leaping to their feet with applause. Miss Conception's one-woman, live singing shows, launched new each year in Puerto Vallarta, Mexico and Provincetown Massachusetts, parody and celebrate some of the greatest characters, movies and TV shows of our time, featuring on-stage transitions from one character to another, with costume change that happen before your eyes.

Mistress Detta

I am a Diva! One of the oldest Diva's around Evansville Indiana, United States. I have been performing since 1989. My name is taken from one of the best Madonna songs. I took that name because although I may seem sweet and nice, I am a very strict Mistress at times on stage. I love to perform and have been known to be a bit over the top on stage. I perform at times at Someplace Else Night Club, and I have been known to take it on the road. I am one of the few who actually take requests when it comes to songs I perform. Though I have never taken a crown, I am happy to just make my fans smile.

Mizz Ladasha

Mizz Ladasha is a DRAG entertainer all the way from Pittsburgh, Pennsylvania, United States! She has been twirling around since 2016, after taking a rebranding break during the pandemic, she re-emerged into the land of Twitch! Ladasha is a horror enthusiast, video game lover, and all-over punk rock DIVA. She is a member of the legendary DRAG team on Twitch STREAMQUEENS. Mizz Ladasha has helped raise over a million dollars alongside fellow streamers for charity organizations all over the world. You can keep up with Mizz Ladasha on all social media platforms! Under "Mizz_Ladasha" and you can follow their Twitch journey and gameplay at twitch.tv/mizz_Ladasha.

It's time to check out
DRAG411.com

Mo B. Dick

Mo B. Dick, DRAG King Legend, MC extraordinaire, show producer, and DRAG King historian, is cited as one of the founding fathers of the modern-day DRAG King movement. Mr Dick, began in November 1995 in the East Village of New York City, New York, United States. He produced and hosted Club Casanova, the world's first weekly party, dedicated solely to DRAG Kings. In 1998, 2001 and 2002, Mo took the Men of Club Casanova on the road to tour US and Canada, which was another first for DRAG Kings. Mo was featured in indie films: Pecker by John Waters, Terror Firmer by Troma, Gendernaughts by Monika Treut, History Lessons by Barbara Hammer. And he was in the documentaries: Venus Boyz by Gabriel Baur, Sex2K: DRAG Kings for MTV, God Shave the Queen for HBO. In 2018, Mo co-created https://DRAGkinghistory.com/ which is being archived in US Library of Congress. For more than 25 years, Mo B. Dick has been the subject of books, documentaries, articles, periodicals, podcasts and more on DRAG Kings proving he is a force to reckon with. http://mrmobdick.com/

Mona Lotz

I have enjoyed entertaining others, even if I wasn't supposed to since childhood. I gained a love for character creation with the use of makeup and prosthetics during my years of acting and singing in theater productions. The creation of Mona was something that has allowed me to be me and love who I am inside and out. As of recent, she is my mouthpiece where I actively tell my story of being raised in a strict religious upbringing and taught that I am wrong for who I am. Now I can say I am a proud Christian man because of her!

Mondo Millions

Mondo Millions is a Deaf, Black, Trans, disabled DRAG King who creates culturally compelling performances in sign language to music, providing Deaf, Black, Queer representation online and in his local community. Mondo creates virtual content and spoken word/poetry to speak on current issues. He speaks English verbally and has a conversational understanding and usage of sign language, as a direct result of systemic ableism and audism. He hopes to create visibility for the Black, Queer, Disabled community and their unique experiences. He organizes and fundraises for marginalized movements and organizations, and speaks out on topics to increase equity and diversity in the LGBTQ/Queer communities. He uses his platform to unpack the concepts of "realness" and "passing" in gender, and advocates for virtual and in-person entertainment to be accessible. His work has been seen worldwide as a result of his work with the first Deaf DRAG show, Handsync. He is proud to be part of the Haus of Flamboyance, an all nonbinary, disabled DRAG haus led by Sir Vix in Sacramento, California, United States. Sacramento is his favorite city, and he is fortunate to share life with his girlfriend and his dog as he pursues his day time career as an intersectional librarian.

Monica Layne

Monica Layne "The Big, The Bold, and the Beautiful; 1978 to the present; from Texas, to DC, to Atlanta, Georgia, United States and all points in between. Entertainer, cast member, emcee, and Show director; proud to have worked beside some of the best in the business. *Photo Credit: Clint Steib*

Morgan Davis

Morgan Davis, The Glitter Queen. Southwest Florida's original bearded DRAG Queen and "Mother Beard" to the current generation of beardiful babes. My career spans thirty years and I live in Cape Coral, Florida, United States. I was the first ever (known) crowned bearded Queen in the country. I owned and produced the first bearded DRAG pageant in 2017. I was emeritus to Miss Florida Bearded Queen and I was one of the original three emeritus to National Bearded Empress. I was show director at the largest club of any kind here in Southwest Florida and I used my platform to bring bearded DRAG to the mainstream. I fought the resistance from the critics in order to create a path for those that came behind me and did not have the place to find support of their art. I have beardiful followers all over the world and I am honored to have been able to shine the spotlight on them as I face retiring from it. Be BEARDIFUL.

Mr. Killin Ya Softly

I been doing DRAG since 1992 to present, so thirty years. Started DRAG in Indianapolis, Indiana, United States at The Ten. My DRAG name was Lil Romeo but my DRAG name is now a play off my actual name. Mr. Killin Ya Softly is just that, a romantic old soul. DRAG for me was a way to see myself as I felt. In 2017 I finally realized I could become who I am today, I am a Proud Trans man who now performs fully as I have always seen myself. I love the stage, the communities, courts I have been part of, performers and families I have made over the years. I love performing anything from Rhythm & Blues to Country. I look forward to traveling to more stages and communities!

Mrs. Chastity Cage

Hello everyone! My name is Mrs. Chastity Cage. I am a Canadian representing the bearded Queens from London, Ontario, Canada. As an appointed minister for my church, I do all sorts of work with the community including providing officiant services for 2SLGBTQIA+ weddings and working with our youth to provide a safe and happy environment for all. I am a crafty Queen and a sort of mad hatter, I have made a hat/fascinator for every occasion. My DRAG daughters are proud to rock their beards and represent the Haus of Cage by my side. Never be afraid to be who you are, no matter who that may be. You can follow me on most forms of social media @mrs.chastitycage! Tik Tok is my favourite, don't tell anyone!

MysterySA

MysterySA is a non-binary alternative DRAG King based in San Antonio, Texas, United States. Due to the pandemic and eventual agoraphobia, they are primarily a Digital DRAG King now. Their art and craft have only grown despite their disabilities. They sew/craft a majority of their DRAG and always doing their best to provide and fight for a space for Digital DRAG artists. If you'd like to see more of their digital DRAG artistry, it can be found through RealMysterySA either on TikTok or Twitch.

Check out the book
DRAG Stories
From DRAG411

Neeko Mac

Neeko Mac (Pretty Boi) born and raised in Arkansas is one of five founding members of the King troupe, Kings of the Springs, Hot Springs, Arkansas, United States. He loves to be out of the box and do performances with music that many wouldn't such as "Man of constant sorrow" from the film "O Brother, Where Art Thou?". He tries hard to bring his guitar playing and vocal talent to the stage as well as being comedic. His favorite song he has ever performed to is "I Wanna Boi" by PWR BTTM. His favorite venue to perform at is Maxine's Live in Hot Springs. His biggest influences are Stevie Nicks, Johnny Cash, and Elvis. His highest hope is to be known as the nicest, most caring, and professional King in the game. He wants to be the best he can possibly be and hopes that he can be inspiring to other Kings who are scared of not being masculine enough. DRAG to him, is the expression and pride of one's true self.

Nemesis

I'm 27 years old from Seattle, Washington, United States. I'm the founder of the Coven of Kindness, the alternative show Taboo, and snatched the Title Ms. Bearvasion 2021. I identify as queer, non-binary, and pansexual. I perform primarily in Seattle and Portland but I have a yearly resident booking at Bearvasion in Salt Lake City. I champion the weird and different in life and want and want people to see something in my art and know that they can embrace and love themselves for who they are.

Learn A Term: EOY
Entertainer of the Year

Nick D'Cuple

Nick D'Cuple is the King of all Kings that represent Southwest Florida. He was the first DRAG King to enter a six-week long competition against DRAG queens for a local competition called DRAG Search in 2021 and snatched the crown! "The most unfortunate thing that happens to people are that they limit themselves by becoming afraid to try anything new. Give yourself a chance!" He is also the founder of a company called A Haus of DRAG and the creator of a competition called Mr & Mrs SWFL DRAG Competition. Both of which are the foundation to express, and include all forms of DRAG, as well as all walks of life. Nick thanks the entertainment director Tara Newhole & Rascals of Fort Myers for giving him the chance to showcase his art in DRAG. Nick is supported and loved by his LGBT community, as well as his family, and DRAG husband, Dik Carrier. Photo Credit: Blackrose Photography

Nikki Ontolodge Monet

Nikki Ontolodge Monet is an old school DRAG Queen, who is still willing to change and grow with the times. Survived the HIV/AIDS epidemic; lost many good friends and chosen family. Was a regular cast member of Pearl's Girls (1987-1990) at the Embers Avenue here in Portland, Oregon and was also a regular cast member of Thursday Night Follies "the Girleens" at Club Arena in Eugene Oregon from (1989-1991). She has lived in Longview, Washington, Hillsboro, Oregon, Portland, Oregon, Eugene, Oregon, and Seattle, Washington. She is 55 years old, but only feels about 35.

Nikki Stone

Nikki Stone is an original member of the GLAMAZONS, an art centered DRAG troupe in Columbus, Ohio, United States. She's sexy, she's scary, and yeah, she's a dude! Nikki's been bearded since 2018, but has been performing in DRAG since 2007 and started burlesquing in 2015! You can find her on Instagram and TikTok @missnikkistone and @peterbiltandstone with Mitze Peterbilt for astrology-related humor!

Nikolette Kilz

Nikolette (Envy) Kilz is a Western Missouri, United States DRAG Queen making her mark throughout the Kansas City and Springfield areas. She has competed in the Miss Gay Wichita Newcomer Pageant, her DRAG mother Tania Carrington's DRAG Race, as well as performing in the Missi B's performance at KC Pride Fest. When the pandemic of 2020 hit, she teamed up with her sisters to form the Haus of Dollz, where they launched online draglesque shows highlighting iconic performers of the troupe. The link to their Pride show STAY PROUD can be found on Nikolette Kilz Instagram page biography. Producing the Pride show is one of her proudest moments, it is an example of the passionate entertainer she tries hard to be.

Check out the DRAG scripts
Best Said Dead
And the play Following Wynter
From DRAG411

Norma Llyaman

I am Norma Llyaman, aka Jim McCoy. This stage-frightened, Bohemian, eccentric performer has been delighting audiences and wayward souls for the past two decades. Vaudeville meets Sideshow, Norma is a crowd favorite. Though her rose is second-hand, she finds every spotlight and freshens the cocktails with her burly burlesque cabaret charisma. Norma is Fanny Brice, Ethel Merman and everyone's favorite Auntie all baked into one delicious Bundt cake. Her live, onstage, and social media adventures are comedic, campy and crazier than most have ever seen. Norma dedicates every show to making people laugh, smile and drink like there is no tomorrow!

Nyxx

Hello, it's me your non-binary weirdo Nyxx. I hail from Fargo, North Dakota, United States. I have been doing DRAG for over ten years. I like to push boundaries living in a red state and encourage everyone to live their own truth. I am a disabled Queen and I encourage visibility with disabilities in our community. I work with multiple organizations in the area. I like to continue to promote positivity in our community and help others in the area to find programs that help find them job placement housing and assistance. Remember, we all walk our own path; it's how we break down barriers and open doors for our future. You can find me on Instagram @nyxx_of_fargo for booking information you can email me at wickliffe.aj@gmail.com.

Hope you are meeting new entertainers From around the world of Different types of DRAG!

Oliver Clozoff

Oliver Clozoff is a character King from South Dakota, United States. After performing for five years, he finally found his way and embraced his theatrical side. Self-titled as the conductor of the hot mess express, this King loves to make people smile, laugh, and have a good time. He'll leave you wondering "how does he bend like that?" as he dips into his gymnastics background! Not one to ever take it easy, he enjoys pushing the envelope as he finds new numbers, new make-up, new costumes, and new ideas as he listens to music or watches movies. He is a member of the all Queer, all Inclusive troupe, VeauxDevil Cabaret. He's charmingly awkward and ready to melt your hearts.

Oliver Steerpike

I was born into a family of football players, United States Marines, musicians and teachers. I'm the first mixed blood American in my family. My family is English and Scottish with a touch of Creole. After a long music career, I went into USMC. Now that I'm back, I see the whole DRAG scene has blown up into all kinds of DRAG. I'm excited because all the stereotypical rules went out the window while I was gone. I was the Closet Ball winner in 92-93 by Sacramento's Court of Love and Confused Gender. Ever since I've performed DRAG, I've been hooked. It's so incredibly liberating. I wish everybody could experience the feeling. I'm a DRAG orphan but I've learned so much over the years. My extreme amount of stage experience from music came in really handy. I show up prepared. I help others and I'm always feeling out the audience to see what's impressing them. I will pick out the song I think will go best with the crowd. I always have three songs ready to perform at all times. I'm easy to work with, and my songs are picked by the average age in the crowd. DRAG is a wonderful thing. I work as a creative consultant for performers, but I am always happy to sit in at a moment's notice. I'm Oliver Steerpike, King of lost DRAG souls!

Onyx Reigns

Onyx Reigns (They/them) is a New Hampshire, United States based DRAG performer bringing social commentary, mystique and a unique brand of body positivity. In addition to their appearance as a featured performer in Planned Parenthood's Northern New England Showcase, Onyx has performed with the Queen City Cabaret of New Hampshire and has been featured on the west coast-based DRAG show, Them Fatale. Mx. Reigns is the creator and host of the Black Legends Revue, in which they provide a digital platform for the talents of Black DRAG and burlesque performers nationwide Onyx believes that all life is a performance, so let's give it all we got.

Operetta St. Sharpe

Operetta St. Sharpe has only been in the DRAG scene for a little over a year and a half and she has loved every second of it. She's from St. Louis, Missouri, United States and is 22 years old. She is the daughter of Cape Girardeau, Missouri queen, Trinity St. Moore, and the sister to Rocky St. Moore. She strives to perform as a theatrical and fun queen. She loves performing songs from musical theatre and from Disney! Operetta just loves the caring and compassionate environment that DRAG has brought her. She also loves the confidence DRAG has given her as a performer. She can't wait to perform again every chance she gets!

Paisley Parque

Paisley Parque is a fifty-year-old trans entertainer from Kernersville, North Carolina, United States. She has been performing for the last 32 years. Paisley has won over thirty titles including five state level titles. She has placed top twelve at four national pageants. Paisley hosts one of North Carolina's longest running DRAG Shows "The Sex Kitten Round Up". She has served on several Pride boards and is very active in the community. Paisley is lovingly known as "The Lips of NC" and is the matriarch of the Parque family. Photo Credit: *Zach Leonard*

Papi Churro

San Francisco Bay Area based Two-Spirit Indigenous DRAG King. Newly transplanted by way of Austin, Texas, United States. DRAG King for over six years, Show Producer for over five years. Co-Producer of such shows as Boyz of Austin, Divinas, Toybox ATX, etc. Founder and Producer of Bizarre Stripper Burlesque, Austin's Premier All Trans Burlesque Troupe. Current member of Nine Inch Males and Om Nom Nom Burlesque. Currently Co-Producing with Om Nom Nom Burlesque and Bizarre Stripper Bay Area. Photo Credit: *Devlin Shand Photography*

Contact DRAG411 if you notice a name of a deceased DRAG performer missing on the DRAG Memorial posted at DRAG411.com/

Paris Grande

Paris Grande, DRAG Icon, Legend and Star. The flippin' & whippin' Pop Princess. British-Bajan Barbie, Lip-sync Assassin and that bitch! Known for the tightest tuck, phattest padded ass, tiniest waist, longest human hair, biggest heels and the highest energy performance guaranteed. Paris has been performing professionally in DRAG for three years, but has dabbled in female transformation as young as eight years old at a local festival. A trained dancer and musical theatre lover, Paris is the intersection of pop, theatre and fashion. Inspired by icons Paris Hilton & Ariana Grande, she takes being a pop diva to a whole new level. You can follow Paris' career on her Instagram where she has an avid and active following of over 20k. @theparisgrande.

Parris B. Cbello

Parris B. Cbello currently resides in Northern Virginia, United States as a member of the Bottoms DRAG family, daughter to the matriarch herself, Ophelia Bottoms. She was on the forefront of femme entertainment in the earlier stages before femme entertainers were really accepted. Winning one of the first nationally recognized titles, she has since been affiliated with Pride and charity work, as well as the Imperial Court of Washington D.C. and has been seated on judge's panels for several systems including EOY and Continental prelims. She focuses more now on keeping femme entertainment valid and visible, while doing her best to aide and assist other femme entertainers who have a passion for the art.

acting.

Patrice Knight

Patrice Knight emerged during my time in the United States Army. My roommate, at the time, took me to my first DRAG Show and I was then put into makeup by the reigning Texas EOY Crystal Starr along with a wig and a cute outfit. I performed "Forever Your Girl." I went on to be known as one of the best Tina Turner Impersonators in Florida. I put up the heels and wigs in 2009 to pursue a career in

Patricia Del Rosario

Hello! My name is Patricia Del Rosario and I am a Queen hailing from Denver, Colorado. I got into DRAG as this art form is a weapon that I use to fight The Patriarchy and Toxic Masculinity. I also believe, at least for me and the way I do it, that it is an art form that empowers feminism. I have found the DRAG community here in Denver loving and supportive and when the time is right, I will happily fight for these people I love. Until then, I'll continue making the world a better place with my chosen art form. *Photo Credit: Danielle Mary*

Check out the
The DRAG Book
From DRAG411

Philli Mi Up

Philli Mi Up is a non-binary DRAG Activist living in Birmingham, England, United Kingdom. You will most likely find Philli giving a lecture, taking part in a protest or just banging on about any social injustice. Outside of DRAG they are a university lecturer specializing in LGBTQIA+ Health and Dementia Care. Philli has more recently started to write poetry based on their queer identity and their research. Philli is involved in working groups, immersive education projects and international projects all with a focus on LGBTQIA+ practice and teaching. Philli is experienced in and open to taking speaking, hosting and poetry bookings, mainly for events such as: Prides, conferences and charitable events. The topics Philli covers are: LGBTQIA+ Ageing, Healthcare, Dementia, Education and inequalities (This list is not exhaustive). Philli is happy to work internationally, delivering talks on Zoom or other online platforms. If you're interested in following Philli's work and/ or making a booking please follow them on Instagram: @PHILLI_MI_UP.

Piranha Del Rey

Piranha Del Rey is a DRAG queen, vocalist and pastel showgirl with a punk rock attitude from Nashville, Tennessee, United States. Proud father the Haüs of Virgö, Piranha tries to positivity impact the scenes that she is in and is constantly trying to uplift other entertainers. Piranha has been doing DRAG sense 2015 and is a non-binary/trans person. She is very vocal on issues in the community and fights for her marginalized siblings. She is very vocal about her bipolar disorder and alcoholism and works on spreading awareness and ending the stigma with those mental health issues and others that don't affect her. She is unapologetically proud of her city and family. You can follow her across platforms at xxpiranhadelrey.

Poppa Pimple

Performing on stages across central Kentucky, United States since they were a child, Poppa Pimple brings a bit of spice to the scene in Lexington. Genderqueer and kink-friendly, Poppa's acts are known to push the boundaries of DRAG and performance. Outside of DRAG, they are a gardener, crafter, and activist. Hailing from Frankfort, Kentucky, Poppa is an avid lover of the arts. Beginning their DRAG career only last October, they still have a lot of growing and finding themselves to do. They specialize in things that make folks squeamish, everything from fake pimples to detailed burn makeup applications. They strive to make people think about their surroundings, and reimagine what DRAG can be. For bookings, contact on Facebook at Poppa Pimple.

Prince Bentley Black

Prince Bentley Black is a country, sweetheart and cinematic, dark, pop, kind of guy based out of Arizona, United States. He was not always a Black, but was adopted into the haus of orphans by his parent's Black Widow and Justin Deeper-Love. Prince Bentley Black has been doing DRAG for five years but took a small break after his first pageant. He is back tearing up the stage and bringing light to his name. After taking time off the stage, he had time to grow and better his performances by bringing more energy. He's expanding his horizons as he performs more and is performing in many new places. He plans to start doing pageants, performs more so he can share what he has learned and to bring joy to the crowds. Prince Bentley Black used to teach a DRAG 101 class at the EON, a clubhouse for the homeless LGBTQ teens. He's growing as a performer and expanding his horizons but also educating and sharing knowledge about the LGBTQ community and DRAG with everyone around him.

Prince Zaddy

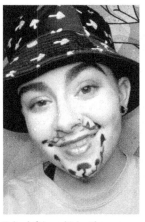

Prince Zaddy (he/they) is a trans DRAG King in Denver, Colorado, United States. They started performing in DRAG eighteen months ago as a way to explore gender and start dancing on stage again. What started as dance focused performance has turned into a whole experience as he grows in his use of theatrical concepts, props, makeup, and stupidity. They chose the name Zaddy because he's always been the "dad friend" in the group, and already responded to Daddy or Zaddy! Zaddy currently hosts a monthly show with their partner/DRAG brother George Not-Strait! You can find them @reannaholmey on Instagram.

Princess DieAnna

My name is Princess DieAnna, the People's Princess. My current home is Tulsa, Oklahoma, United States and is originally from Ft. Collins, Colorado. I started practicing the art of bearded DRAG in 2018. My passion for an androgynous look and dedication to diversity is what fuels my fire. I was crowned as the Inaugural Oklahoma's Bearded Queen in May 2022. My goal in DRAG is to foster inclusiveness, spread kindness, and show the world just how beautiful being bearded is. Please find me on Facebook as Princess DieAnna and Instagram as Princess_Dieanna.

Are you a DRAG Performer?
Get on the DRAG411 group on facebook
(not the page) to get your DRAG profile in the
2023 International "Who's Who of DRAG" Directory

Prinze Valentino

Prinze Valentino is Genderfuckery Royalty. Named #1 DRAG King in Los Angeles, California, United States by LA Blade Magazine, his stage presence is intoxicating and his energy is fierce! When Prinze performs, it's personal. He takes his audience on a powerful journey full of emotion and passion in hopes of empowering others to be confident in their most authentic, beautiful selves. Prinze has spoken on panels, performed throughout the Midwest & California, and co-led Cincinnati's queer Burlesque & DRAG troupe, "Smoke & Queers," which provides a safe space for the LGBTQIA+ community to embrace their creativity. This non-binary King has been kicking ass in LA since July 2021. *Photo Credit: Abraham Ramos*

PurrZsa Kyttyn Azrael

Mrs. PurrZsa Kyttyn Azrael, (My'Chyl Purr) known as "The Star of Stage and Screen" first graced the DRAG stage in late 1993. Since then, he has captured over twenty titles. With a Bachelor of Arts in Acting from University of Tennessee/Knoxville, United States; he is a literal Drama Queen. He has appeared as the DRAG lead in "The Legend of Georgia McBride" along with multiple tv and movie performances. There is really only one word to describe him, "Committed". He is committed to giving a good show. He has been committed to his partner since 1996. If you know him at all, you know he should probably be committed.

It's time to check out
DRAG411.com

Qaptain

Your "Captain-with-a-Q," aka Kit Boulter (they/them) is a multidisciplinary performer who lives, works, and plays outside of "gender norms" bringing visibility and representation of non-binary individuals and art. They have been appearing in DRAG professionally for five years, but they started decades ago in cosplay, musical theatre, and expression through song, digital media and visual art. A real-life Captain, they work as a pirate, a poet, and an advocate for trans rights and safety in urban and rural communities. You can find them singing, playing, and dancing on stages and screens across Turtle Island. They call Toronto, Canada (Tkaronto) home, as well as Georgian Bluffs in rural Ontario, and they are always up for an adventure and new horizon. All aboard, Sailors, your Qaptain will sweep you away! Find them @qpt_kit on Instagram and @qaptain on TikTok.

Quinn Tessential

Quinn Tessential is a DRAG King, host, and producer based in Minneapolis, Minnesota. Quinn uses humor and camp to entertain and make the audience laugh. His looks are inspired by '80s men's fashion, active wear, and a combination of the masculine and feminine. Quinn started producing DRAG shows after noticing the lack of diversity in casting in the Twin Cities despite the overwhelming amount of talent in the area.

Photo Credit: derekgphotography

Hope you are meeting new entertainers
From around the world of
Different types of DRAG!

Raquel Summers

Raquel Summers is from Wilmington, Delaware, United States. She started female impersonation back in 2001 and was crowned Miss. 814 Newcomer 2001. After a few years she went into hibernation to reinvent herself and when she came out in 2020, she was crowned Miss. Delaware Valley All Star National and in 2021 was crowned Miss. Lebanon Grand Diva! She has traveled to New York, Pennsylvania, Maryland, And Ohio. She currently hosts a monthly show at Crimson Moon in Wilmington, Delaware. She loves to dance and do Broadway on stage. Just keep an eye out because you never know where she'll pop up next. Muah for now.

Rebel Love Diva

I've been doing DRAG for twelve years. I started for a random turnabout show when all my DRAG mother's guests had canceled for her show. Two friends and I stepped up and donned our wigs and beat our faces to save the day! Ever since, I've performed all over Las Vegas, Nevada and also Los Angeles, California, United States. My most memorable gig was working at Drink and DRAG in downtown Las Vegas. I was surrounded by the top DRAG performers in town and I learned so much! During the pandemic I took a hiatus, as most of us did, but now I'm back and starting my journey to legend status.

Check out our next book
DRAG SHOW
What it takes to get on stage in the beginning

Redd FaFilth

Redd FaFilth, "the GoTHICCC Non-Binary Sensation," is a stage stomping DRAG Monster from San Francisco, California, United States. Even with a short career of only four years, this breakout performer has snatched many titles including 2022 RORSHOK Annus Novus Champion and the 3rd Best Elvira Look-a-like Worldwide. They slay each stage they encounter with spot-on Cosplays, killer makeup looks, and campy humor. Redd FaFilth hopes to be the voice for the little queer weirdos who wish to no longer be confined by the gender binary, to be free to be who they are. With Redd's hunger, drive and determination, this performer is unstoppable! You can follow Redd's journey on all social media platforms @ReddFaFilth, and for other inquiries, please email them: creepscreationsredd@gmail.com. Don't sleep on Redd FaFilth!

Reggie Knight

Reggie Knight is an older yet new King. At 47 years old, he has only been performing for fifteen months. He is the current reigning Mr. King Waterloo 2021 and a proud member of the Cedar Valley Kings in Waterloo, Iowa, United States. He is a King who brings different styles and different genres of music to the stage. He has performed on the main stage at Cedar Valley Pridefest as well as multiple other venues in Iowa. Reggie is always willing to lend a hand and help others in their times of need. *Photo Credit: Stephanie McNally Thome*

DRAG411.com
7,000 Performers in 32 Countries

Remi Storm

Remi Storm, is non-binary and was Mr. JOMO Pride 2021. They have been performing for almost three years and are based out of Joplin, Missouri, United States. They started DRAG as a way to express their masculinity. The inspiration for Remi's name came from their favorite Disney Movie Ratatouille, a rat who didn't give up on his dreams no matter the challenge. Remi has numerous disorders and DRAG is a way to escape that reality. Remi has a rare brain disorder called Functional Neurological Disorder which means Remi can have seizures. Remi also has Tourette's Syndrome which causes tics, which can be unwanted movements or vocal sounds. Remi has had to learn to re-walk twice, but even with the challenges that Remi faces on a daily, they are a very happy person to be around, in fact, it's hard to slow Remi down because they are always going at high speed.

Robin Yablind

He'll steal your girl, your man, and possibly your heart, because he's Robin Yablind! Robin is known across Aotearoa (New Zealand) for his engaging draglesque acts, and while sexually confusing the audience has become a specialty, it's his cheeky performance style that will win you over. Robin has collected multiple New Zealand Burlesque titles, including Mister Burlesque Aotearoa 2018, and is currently reigning Supreme Grand Tease. In the Supreme Grand Tease Finals, Robin Yablind was the first performer ever to take the title in every category: Best Classic, Best Neo and Best Improv! They are also a founding member of Wellington's own Draglesque troupe, the Haus of Sin, and are a core cast member of the first ever DRAG musical for children - The Glitter Garden. When not on stage, the person behind Robin Yablind, Niko, teaches burlesque and dance classes at Studio L'amour Wellington, and has a particular interest in translating movement for everybody. Find Robin contouring those abs, sharpening his brows, or on socials at @robin_yablind (Instagram) @robinyablindnz (Facebook). *Photo Credit: Jeff Tollan Photography*

Robyn Valentine

My name is Robyn Valentine and I'm known locally in my city of Corpus Christi, Texas, United States as the Queen of Downtown. I discovered the art of DRAG by flipping through the TV channels and stumbling across a little show known as RuPaul's DRAG Race. Though confused by what I saw, I was immediately intrigued! Slowly I began practicing makeup on myself behind closed doors until the day came that I could elevate my craft by performing, hosting, and show organizing. This June marks ten years since I began my journey and I've managed to accomplish so many big things! Since the beginning, my goals were clear, I wanted to bring DRAG out of the bars and into the mainstream by offering events at venues outside of bars, all ages events, earlier events, and as many free shows as I could. I want our art to be accessible regardless of age, sexuality, income, etc. The response to my efforts has been unbelievable. I've received so many messages from people who never had seen a show before, people who bring their families, and even the occasional person who brings along a less than accepting companion who ends up enjoying themselves. I want to go all the way with my craft and I am fueled now more than ever to succeed.

Rocky St. Moore

My name is Rocky St. Moore, that's Rocky like the boxer! I am still new when it comes to DRAG; I've only been performing a few years. I started performing in Missouri, United States, and got adopted by Trinity St. Moore. I love DRAG because I have never felt freer than when I am on stage. DRAG has helped me become who I am and it really helped me when it came to fully coming out of the closet. I feel like I'm one with the music whenever I perform. I am always trying to do something different with my DRAG style and performance. The people I have met along the way have become my family, and I am so excited to see what the future holds. You can follow me on Facebook and Instagram @rockystmoore and DM me for bookings on either site.

Roi Griffin

Roi Griffin is a timeless witch who travels between the doom and the glam. Express themselves breaking through mind, bones, blood and soul with a sacred mixture of masculine and feminine energies with no boundaries. Servant of fire, practice their magic embodying and giving out the Goddess/God energy to help others to elevate the consciousness of this world; the arts and the love are the only roads to touch the human heart so they perform to transcend time and stay forever in collective memory. Tarot, astrology, singing, theater, make up and DRAG conforms this entity developing magnetic performances and a stunning presence. You can find them as @roigriffin across the entire internet!

Romeo Casanova

Romeo Casanova by night as a lip-syncing and dancing DRAG King performing '90s to now of all genres of music since 2002. By day, I work in the behavioral health field with children and adults serving the community. Being a DRAG King entertainer over the last twenty years, I have seen the world of "DRAG" and the entertainment aspect evolve immensely. It is amazing to see all kinds of valid entertainment on stage as it needs to evolve into its own and everyone deserves a place onstage, even old-timers like me! *Photo Credit: @DaLani Visual*

Romeo DeMornay Sanchez

I'm Romeo DeMornay Sanchez, aka Mr. Kneez from Des Moines, Iowa, United States. I got that nickname because I'm always bouncing all over the place. You can catch me climbing on a bar, table or chair. I just like to move; some say a little more than the camera can keep up with. The crowd is where you will find the energy! Catch me at one spot in the venue, blink and see me on the other side. I am the show director, host and one of the original members of the Kapital City Kings. A show cast member at The Garden Restaurant and Show Lounge. I'm also a show cast member of Covered in Melanin at The Legendary Blazing Saddle. Voted East Village's Best DRAG King 2021.

Rory Phoenix Monroe

Rory Phoenix Monroe is 28 Years old transgender female to male. Has been performing in and around Cedar Rapids, Iowa, United States for the last two years and doesn't plan on stopping. He has won Mr. Key City Pride pageant in 2021 and plans to run in 2023 for the trans pageant in Wisconsin. He is also a member of the Cedar Valley Kings as of 2021 and joined the House of Monroes in 2021 as well. After June, some goals for the remainder of the year will be to travel to some states and perform there as well. Most of his music is punk pop, and alternative music, when given the chance he will do his best to find creepy songs and do themes for Friday the 13th or Halloween, which includes fake blood. He does ask the host to put a warning out for those who are not okay with it. But every now and then Rory likes to spice it with some Hispanic music for his heritage. Originally from Chicago, Illinois but happily a resident in Cedar Rapids, Iowa. Check him out soon; you definitely won't regret it. If you want a hug, he isn't opposed to giving them. Rory absolutely loves giving out hugs. If you aren't comfortable with asking, hint with your arms, and he will ask you instead. *Photo credit: Angie May Brown*

RuPaul

RuPaul is one of America's most famous DRAG queens, achieving a cross-over appeal that changed the face of entertainment. He became a supermodel, and even launched The RuPaul Show on VH1. Throughout his appearances in film and on television, RuPaul continued to release additional albums as a singer. RuPaul appeared on a number of television series. In addition to his work on television and in film, RuPaul is the author of a number of books. RuPaul has been very public about his opinion regarding gender-specific pronouns, since he often appears in the female form in DRAG, but also as "himself." He has made it clear that he is perfectly satisfied with either pronoun as a reference, and he often appears outside of his DRAG persona to host his current shows, RuPaul's DRAG Race and RuPaul's DRAG U, both of which can be found on VH1. Book RuPaul through bookingentertainment.com. *Photo Credit: David Shankbone*

Russell Mania

I'm a non-binary performer, KJ, comedian, host and I produce the Bling Showcase. I started off in 1987 as a DRAG performer named Tuesdae Knyte. I live in Lakeland, Florida, United States with my husband of 32 years. I'm a comic performer and impersonate Elton John and Cartman from South Park. Photo Credit: Louis Cooper

DRAG411.com
7,000 Performers in 32 Countries

Ryder Royal Storm

Ryder Royal Storm started performing as a DRAG King in 2019 in Springfield, Missouri, United States. He has returned to his hometown Norman, Oklahoma where he performs, including surrounding areas. He travels to different cities and states to bring a positive message of love and inclusion. He is a positive, uplifting, high energy King that plans to keep this Storm rolling for years to come.

Sabastian Taylor

Sabastian Taylor is a Pennsylvania, United States native. He has performer for 21 years. His career started when he entered a local club competition and took home the title. He has held numerous titles over the years but lives for the passion of performance, not the crowns. Sabastian's performances are known to extend across all genres and has audiences craving more from his dance moves, sex appeal to his comedic antics. *Photo Credit: Michael Roston*

Sabrina LaVey

College Station, Texas, United States. Sabrina has been doing DRAG for just over half a year, and in this time, she has proven that with enough practice, determination, and drive it doesn't matter how long you've been doing something you can be just as good as the pros. She's competed in Halo's DRAG U (in Bryan, Texas) and got second runner up in her first ever DRAG competition. Her style is very pop princess and will always be the loudest girl in the room! Her goal through DRAG is to show the world that no matter who you are, or what you come from, that there is a place for you. You can follow her on Instagram at sabrina_lavey_.

Salma Love Taylor

Born Mexican, migrated to America in 2009, and my DRAG career started March 2018. I'm part of Haus of Taylor. The creation of Salma Love Taylor started when I was diagnosed with chronic pain due an old work injury. DRAG was an escape from my darkness days. I enjoy DRAG so much; it literally changed my life. I'm part of an amazing community that supports all types of performers. I get to see many types of DRAG and learn along the way as I travel around the east coast of Florida.

Santana Romero

My name is Santana Romero, DRAG King royalty from Toledo, Ohio. I have performed all over the Midwest and pride myself on my versatile movement style and impersonations. I love to captivate the audience with my high energy numbers and leave you wanting a little more with each performance. I've been gliding across stages for eleven years and counting. I love nothing more than to inspire others through this art form by passing down the knowledge I've learned by being part of this community.

Learn A Term: FTM/MTF
Transitioned Female to Male
Transitioned Male to Female

Sara Hearts

Hi, I'm Sara Hearts out of Tulsa, Oklahoma, United States. I've been doing the art of female impersonation for about twelve years now. I have performed in many clubs in Oklahoma, Texas, Missouri, and Florida. I enjoy traveling around entertaining and meeting new people. I've had many opportunities to do what I love. Three years ago, I started a new journey of life and I've started doing hormones. I can't wait for what the future hasn't stored for me.

Sassy Black

Hi, I'm Sassy Black. I live in Tallahassee, Florida, United States. My moto is. "Life's too short, live it to the fullest." I'm the host of Hot Friday Night Party at 926 Bar & Grill in Tallahassee. I started my DRAG career in 2005 in Key West, Florida where I worked at Aqua Night Club and also 801 Bourbon Bar. I love to make people laugh and have fun, inspire others to be themselves and love everyone for who they are. In 2007, I was Key West Miss Closetball, 2012. I was Key West Miss Pride, 2014 Key West Miss Mardi Gras of Bourbon St. Email me at Sassyblack2@gmail.com. Instagram/Sassyblack2

Check out the book
Spotlight Today
From DRAG411

Saváge Fierce

My name is Saváge Fierce, located in Fort Myers, Florida, United States. I first started doing DRAG in 2018 and have continued to evolve and change myself to find the mold that she can thrive in. She sings, she dances, she's spooky, she's glamorous. Saváge was born in a way to channel the fierce feminine energy I have, and as a well to balance gender dysmorphia. She's a fighter and ever evolving. I strive to continue to fight for the idea that all DRAG is valid, because it is art baby. Follow me on Instagram at @savagefierceswfl!

Savannah L Judd

Savannah L Judd is Northern Kentucky's very own country girl. I have been performing and entertaining for fourteen years. I am best known for my big heart, my fun-loving spirit, my love of country music, and my "Bitch In The Kitchen" dinner parties. I was the last DRAG daughter of the Legendary Darlene Love (Cincinnati, Ohio, United States). I have hosted and/or show directed at numerous locations in the Ohio-Indiana-Kentucky area, including Club Bronz, Shooters Bar, Simon Says and Pirate's Den Bar and Grill in Cincinnati, Ohio; L'Burgs Drinks & More in Lawrenceburg, Indiana; The Hot Spot, Mac's Pizza Pub and The Cellar Bar Restaurant Venue (currently show director) in Northern Kentucky. I am the emeritus to Miss Gay Cincinnati, Ohio. Biggest inspirations include Wynonna Judd, Reba McEntire, Gretchen Wilson, Miranda Lambert and Kelly Clarkson. Find me on Facebook or Instagram, or catch me all over the Tri-State area! *Photo Credit: Scott Dittgen*

Saylor Alexander Vontrell

I'm Saylor Alexander Vontrell from Birmingham, Alabama, United States. I've been working in the art of DRAG for ten years. I am currently Alabama National Showman 2022 and Mister Arkansas USofA MI 2019-22. I love to travel and constantly looking for new places to express my art.

Scarlet Sinderella

Scarlet Sinderella is a bearded beauty who originally comes from Evansville, Indiana, United States, but now resides and entertains in Lakeland, Florida. Scarlet prides herself on being humble and is the self-proclaimed "America's Bearded Sweetheart". Scarlet loves to raise money for LGBTQ+ charities and works a lot with "the Rose Dynasty Foundation, Inc." to do so. Though Scarlet is still learning her art, she just wants to make sure people are comfortable with being exactly who they are and enjoying her performances. Eventually she would love to compete in a national pageant. She is the Current Miss. Magnolia 2019-2023 which represents Someplace Else Night Club in Evansville, Indiana. That title will finally be passed on January of 2023. Ricky (Scarlet's boy half) is a Wine Tender and loves to learn as much as he can about wine. Give him a crisp Sauvignon Blanc and you may just become best friends. Whether she is giving you Broadway or white trash Barbie, you are sure to be entertained! Find her on Instagram at @beardrr93! She's beauty, she's grace, she has hair on her face! *Photo Credit: Charles Wolf Photography*

Scarlett Dailey

Scarlett Dailey performed in 29 states and held over 96 titles over a 32-year career. Appearing in three movies and enjoys traveling. I am thankful for the opportunities that DRAG allowed me. I was crowned Miss Gay World 85-86 and worked at the number one show bar, Lavitas in Atlanta, Georgia, United States. I retired from show business while it still had the wow factor. I now own a rare plant nursery in North Carolina. *Photo Credit: Jose of Durham*

Scrappy Legacy

I am Shay Brewer. Scrappy means full of fighting spirit, and Legacy means the footprints I've made and the service I give to my community. I started on the stage at the age of seventeen, DRAG got me through some dark times. I began volunteering at Oklahoma's for Equality Center, United States for four years and was offered a position. I work with the youth and I'm over Tulsa Pride Entertainment as well as leading a Male Transgender support group. I love being able to give opportunities to anyone that wants to make a difference. It's taken years to become who I am now, but proud to say I love being a mentor, a listener, and role model. I was honored to become The King of Tulsa Pride Emeritus. That was and is the most valuable title I've ever had because it taught me how to serve others and be held accountable and stay humble at all times cause people look up to you and are always watching. I'm your current reigning Mister Gay Oklahoma United States 2021. I also organize the Equality Centers Gala, Pride Bingo, which is a huge banquet where 70 percent of our donors attend. I host the only Successful DRAG King Show in Oklahoma at Club Majestic in Tulsa called "Bad Boys on The Block" for five years now! I bring Kings from all over the country, and I'm a part of the DSM Kings in Iowa. I've Entertained at Pride events across the nation.

Sean Wolff

Sean Wolff was in Topeka, Kansas, United States in 2007 where this King was born. Sean has been involved in many community events and fundraisers including Kansas City Pride, Missouri Gay Rodeo Association board member, Topeka Prom Board, Leather and Lace Ball, Central Plains Leather Contest, The Pulse Nightclub fundraiser, many AIDS fundraisers and the first Women of Drummer Contest. He holds the titles of Rhinestone Cowgirls King 2018, and MsTer Missouri Gay Rodeo Association 2020. Sean has performed across the country from Las Vegas to Missouri. Sean helps others through fundraising and being a mentor/teacher, friend. His most important job is offering an ear to listen or a shoulder in a time of need. He takes great pride and dedication in his performances and completely loves making people smile and have a good time! He has been an inspiration to many performers over the years, first battling his genetic disability, and then starting his transition. He can inspire, coach and sometimes give you that push that you need to go on. Find him at Sean Wolff-Higgins on Facebook, Instagram: Seanwolff76 or seanwolffhiggins76 on TikTok. *Photo Credit: Liz-Ember Allison-Murphy*

Selena Gonzales

Selena Gonzales has been a part of the South West Michigan, United States DRAG scene for 27 years. She graduated in 1995 from Albion, Michigan and started performing at Brothers Beta Club in Kalamazoo, Michigan. She has won Ms. Michigan Gayworld Newcomer and is the current reining Ms. Red Ribbon Professional. After the passing of her sister, Breanna Nacole Fest, she took over as the

Who's Who of DRAG

owner of the Michigan Gayworld pageant which is still going strong today. She is an advocate for Survivor Strong (which raises money for domestic violence victims) and Hope house (which raises money for rehabilitation for drug and alcohol abuse). Ms. Selena is active on Instagram and Facebook.

Shae Snow

Hello you lovely creatures, my name is Shae Snow. I'm the Shesquatch-Queen of Omaha, Nebraska, United States. I began performing in 2017, when I ran for Mr. Midwest Esquire and won to everyone's surprise! From there I won the title of Mr. Flixx (2019) and was a family line member of the Imperial Court of Nebraska (Prince 38). I am a benefit Queen and love to help my community and any community that will have me. By hard work, I have been selected as the DRAG show chair for SEARCH Nebraska (a local leather/kink/fetish education organization). My pronouns are He/They/She/She-Squatch, I've been an on-call emcee for shows and events, a pageant judge, and love performing. If you would like to book me, reach out on Facebook (Shae Snow DRAG Artist) or Instagram (xoxo_shaniasnow_xoxo). I hope to never stop learning about myself and DRAG, and hope even more to meet you in the future! *Photo Credit: Travis Steiff*

Check out the book
DRAG World
From DRAG411

ShaeShae LaReese

ShaeShae LaReese, better known to the world as "Motha Gangsta" is from Laguna Beach, California, United States by way of Puerto Rico. She started shaping the world of DRAG in 1987 after being taught the art of female impersonation while performing as a backup dancer for her DRAG mother, Angel Sheridan. In her 35 years of entertaining, she has captured five national titles as well as numerous awards. Her notable accomplishments include Miss Gay USofA, Miss USofA Classic, Miss National, and Miss Gay United States. She is not only known in the DRAG community as an icon but also as an innovator. Her current titles are Miss Gay 90's, Miss Club Rio, Miss Heart of Florida, and the Southern States National Show Girl. She continues to shape and encourage new and established DRAG in the pageant and show community. She thinks of her DRAG family as the house of misfits and orphans, encouraging those that have come from estranged DRAG families, or those that have retired to come to join her legacy and continue to be a voice and advocate for equality, inclusion, and diversity in the DRAG community. *Photo Credit: Erika Wagner*

Shasta McNastie

Shasta McNastie is my name and old school DRAG is my game. I been entertaining for sixteen years and loving every second of it. Current reigning Miss Stonewall 2021 and a proud sober queen. I believe strongly in community and being kind and loving one another. I started in Topeka, Kansas, and lived in Kansas City, Missouri, United States. I now live in Wilton Manors, Florida.

Shaunna Rai

I'm Shaunna Rai. I consider myself a showgirl. I've been performing for about thirty years. In the '90s, when I was twenty, two trans performers, Ashley and Marlena helped shape who I am today. I'm an advocate for trans rights, equality and HIV/AIDS charities. I perform throughout New England, but call Maine home. I encourage new performers, by answering questions, helping how I can, or giving advice. I believe that DRAG is an artform and all DRAG is valid. I have a few titles and was the first DRAG Queen to Grand Marshall the Pride in the Portland, Maine parade. *Photo Credit: Steve Dixon*

Shego Wylde

Hey y'all! I'm Shego Wylde from Fayetteville, Arkansas, United States. I'm a relatively new Queen (First performance in April 2022) I'm crafty, put everything I have into everything I do and love to dance. I live by the phrase "well I'm gay, so how hard can it be!" I hope to get involved however I can in the local LGBT+ community but haven't quite found my niche yet. My goal with my DRAG is to embody feminine and androgynous power and beauty, and to inspire LGBT+ youth to be themselves however they can. Winner of C4's Just a Taste open talent night April 2022. Follow me on Instagram @Shegowylde

Are you a DRAG Performer?
Get on the DRAG411 group on facebook
(not the page) to get your DRAG profile in the
2023 International "Who's Who of DRAG" Directory

Shelby Fine

Hello, my name is Shelby Fine the "Beautiful Bearded Bimbo" from College Station, Texas, United States. I started DRAG August 2021 and have been rapidly advancing my craft. You can catch me competing in America's Bearded Queen at the national level. I'm part of the fabulous Adonis family from Texas. You can follow me on Instagram @shelbyfine69 or on Facebook as Shelby Queen. Feel free to reach me there for booking information.

Shire Paige

I am Shire Paige, The Hobbit King. Why Hobbits? They're short, love lazy days with a pipe and a book, and have a heavy appreciation for potatoes. Shire is everything I am not in everyday life- outgoing, smooth, almost cocky. Shire is where I learned to be comfortable in my own skin and I enjoy using DRAG to help others do the same. *Photo Credit: Carrie Strong*

Sir Labia

Hi all. My given name is Avelina Verdugo, DRAG name Sir Labia. I'm a 53-year-old human that enjoys DRAG as a form of self-expression. I have a lot of fun creating my shows and love creating characters. I repurpose most of my costumes and love a challenge!

Sir Manther

Sir Manther is an aggressively insecure and preemptively nostalgic '90s kid. He has been giving angsty and earnest DRAG performances throughout Kansas, United States since 2017. A perpetual fan of questionable song covers, unnecessary cartwheels, and parodying the tragicomedy that is gender, Sir Manther's performances span a variety of genres and styles. He doesn't think twice about jumping off stages, climbing on tables, or flipping his way into your heart. Sir Manther loves connecting with queer and trans youth in family friendly venues, but he isn't afraid to explore more adult numbers and is always prepared to engage in some gender-ambiguous nudity. You can count on him for frantic energy, multi-colored facial hair, and edgy trans content. He has performed at Little Apple Pride, Topeka Pride, and Wichita Pride, as well as numerous fundraiser shows, the first ever OKamp for Kansas and Oklahoma queer and trans youth, and made appearances at the Kansas State University homecoming parade.

Sir Vix

Sir Vix is a DRAG King from Sacramento, California, United States. He is the father of the Haus of Flamboyance (an all AFAB, nonbinary, disabled DRAG family) and has been a DRAG King since 2017. He is known for bright color schemes, extravagant suits, and dramatic paints. Sir Vix makes the majority of his clothes, as he has been sewing since he was 13 years old. He was raised in theater by parents who met onstage and feels he has been preparing to be a DRAG King his whole life. His DRAG style aims to challenge toxic masculinity by mixing Daddy and Femboy aesthetics.

Skye G. Bender

Skye G. Bender is a genderbending dream boi based out of Fort Myers, Florida, United States. He has been performing since his debut at Cruiser's in Cape Coral where he became the 2021 Mr. SWFL DRAG King at the annual competition sponsored by A Haus of DRAG. Since holding the crown, Skye has been at various venues in Southwest Florida and he can be found performing, attending, and volunteering at DRAG bingo/karaoke/trivia charity events. Skye is building his song list and looking forward to learning more and getting better at doing his art in DRAG. He likes to keep his audiences both entertained and enlightened, choosing to show them comedy and togetherness by his song choices. Now a member of A Haus of DRAG, Skye loves being part of an all-inclusive group of DRAG performers who strive to support one another in their art.

Spank Knightly

DRAG King, actor, and human cigarette; Spank Knightly has been making DRAG for four years now. He has frequently performed in the central Illinois and Midwest areas as well as Chicago and Boston, and hopes to travel with his DRAG in the near future. Visual arts and makeup art are his forte, drawing inspiration from old cartoons and art deco with some psychedelic and vibrant colors in the mix.

Are you a DRAG Performer?
Get on the DRAG411 group on facebook
(not the page) to get your DRAG profile in the
2023 International "Who's Who of DRAG" Directory

Sparkling Sapphire Carrington

Sparkling is the youngest DRAG Queen in Champaign, Illinois. She has been performing since 2018 and she is now ten years old. Sparkling has always, since a very young age, loved DRAG, makeup, hair, nails. She does her own makeup and hair and wigs. Sparkling perfects everything she sets her mind to. Sparkling also does All Star Cheerleading. When she isn't doing cheerleading, she is practicing for her next DRAG performance. Sparkling, ever since her first performance when Peach from the Midwest Carrington asked if she would be her DRAG daughter, has drawn one of the biggest crowds. Sparkling lived from the age of two to seven years old in Dixon, Illinois and 2021 they had a Pride protest because the city would not let them celebrate Pride. So, they had a protest and Sparkling was the only performer that day and she killed it. The protest got the city of Dixon to have their first ever Pride festival and Sparkling is performing along with lots of others.

Special K

Special K is a part of the Culver House and has been performing in Pennsylvania and Delaware for about eight months. As an androgynous performer, Special K is shy and timid but loves to step out of their comfort zone and show people that you can do anything that you put your mind to it. Special K believes in diversity, equality, inclusion, and enjoys being part of Culver Entertainment, which also believes in the same values and shows the world that, "It's okay."

STACI

A non-binary, live singing, DRAG artist hailing from Long Island, New York., United States They have been spreading their magic throughout Long Island and New York City. Staci's been performing in DRAG for three years. To showcase that it doesn't matter how you identify, you can do drag and showcase your art to the world. Staci's style of DRAG is campy, over the top sequin, and glamour. Staci is known for their powerhouse vocals and their comedic lip sync mixes." *Photo Credit: Phil Chanel*

Star Sirius

Star Sirius shines brightly under the heated lamps of the stage. Their fantasy-style characters and creatures are as expressive and fluid as their gender; so, you will never know quite what to expect next from this dazzling siren. As an artist they are influenced by fantasy, gothic, gore, and horror aesthetics. Sired by none other than the illustrious Ellis D., they have had the privilege to grow in all things truly weird, bizarre, and unapologetically queer.

Starlet Skye

Hello, I'm Starlet Skye dubbed the ultimate showgirl with a career spanning over fifteen years and all over Europe! I moved to the United States in March 2015. Originally British, I have taken southern Florida by storm with a different type of show available with quick wit and attention to details. Winning my first national title in November of 2021 at the first America's Bearded Queen! I am currently touring,

Who's Who of DRAG

promoting the title and building the system. An avid lover of all things theatrical I hope to see you in a town near you soon. Facebook: Skye Beckett or Americasbeardedqueen1@gmail.com.

Steele Macendemhoez

Steele Macendemhoez, a name given to him by a friend because he was drawing blanks on a name, is a legend in Columbus, Ohio. Known mostly as Steele Mac'n, he and his DRAG family helped solidify the DRAG King scene of Ohio in the mid - 2000s. Traveled all over the Southwest and all the way to Toronto. Mac Daddy... Mister swag himself, Steele Macn' is a founding member of the swag-tastic duo known as the Steele Brothers, whose hard hitting, hip hop & rap performances always have the crowd's arms in the air, screaming for more! The Steele Brother's evolved into the Steele Family, once both the brothers grew on the Columbus scene and became DRAG Daddy's. As time went on, Steele Macn finally landed on a name for himself, Daddy Longleggz. The Steele Family still performs hard hitting, get you to your feet performances in the Midwest. And yes, they are still a crowd favorite!! If you ever get the chance to visit Columbus, Ohio ... they are troupe or even a solo performance you do not want to miss.

Stevie Phoenix

Stevie Phoenix is a high energy, campy DRAG King who isn't afraid of a little glam! Located in southeast Michigan and traveling all over the United States, Stevie brings theatre to the stage, all while placing a priority on activism and breaking down the walls of binary gender. He was crowned Mr. Southbend Tavern King in 2019, Mr. Toledo Gay Pride King in 2019, Mr. Ohio Gay Pride King in 2020, and District West Entertainer of the Year in 2021. Stevie is also the founder and executive chair of Fremont Ohio Pride, a nonprofit

Who's Who of DRAG

organization in his home town of Fremont, Ohio that has established an LGBTQ+ support group, a GSA in the local public high school, holds an annual Pride festival, and has raised money for local domestic violence efforts. He started his DRAG journey in 2017, and through the art of gender performance discovered his own gender identity. Stevie strives to spread his message of kindness, because even though everyone on earth has unique and different experiences, it is through kindness that we can share and educate one another about those experiences. Follow: Facebook: Stevie Phoenix. Instagram: @stevie_phoenix. Twitter: @phoenix_stevie. TikTok: @stevie_phoenix.

Stormy Vain

Stormy Vain, DRAG Queen entertainer for twenty years in the Washington DC, United States metro area. Owner of adult entertainment business, Xrated Candy Pop Up Shop. Charity work includes feeding the homeless and rescuing and placing unwanted pets into new homes.

Summer Lynne Seasons

Summer Lynne Seasons has been entertaining audiences for 25 years in the Portland, Oregon, United States area. She is the proud yearly host of the Gay Pride Parade and enjoys traveling all over the country to perform. Summer has held many titles in Portland but is proudest of being voted Rose Empress 58 and winning LaFemme Magnifique International 2019-2021. She has been working at Darcelle XV Showplace for 14 years now and can often be seen impersonating Stevie Nicks and Adele. *Photo Credit: Carlos Silvas*

Summer Rayne

Bonjour et Bonne Journée! Summer Rayne is The Bearded Bearoness of Houston, Texas, United States. She is a fully self-taught queen, from mixes and costumes, to hair and makeup. She values learning hands on and cherishes DRAG cultural experiences. Summer is a huge advocate on getting in trouble, pushing the limits, and always staying true to themselves. Because Summer's alter ego can work hard, be serious, and seem to follow the rules, once the lashes and nails come on Summer is able to lift the veil and become truly unstoppable! You can find Summer on many different social media platforms. On Facebook, Summer Rayne and on Instagram @thesummerrayne. Summer is available for all bookings, anywhere in the world!

Sylas Crow

My name Iralu Fernandez (born in 1977). As a DRAG King known as Sylas Crow, aka "King of Freaks," a Trans male from the westside of Puerto Rico. Started doing DRAG on December 1st, 2018. As a DRAG King I am queer, freaky with a twist of horror, sensual and love to play with the audience's senses. Always working to help our LGBTTQIA and DRAG community.

Every October we collect the information posted in these books from the DRAG performers. They provide us the information. If someone is missing, it is because they have not sent us their biography and picture... yet. Each book we hope to double in size. This is the first "International Who's Who of DRAG" book.

Tasha Dane

Tasha Dane has been dazzling audiences in Delaware, United States and surrounding states for years and has been a staple to the Delaware DRAG community. She is the quintessential Queen of spins, dips, tricks, and even a little comedy (just the tip). A host and resident diva in the Delaware scene, Tasha believes in the value of all DRAG and in the community it creates. Outside of DRAG, she has served the community in leadership and legal support roles of various LGBTQ+ organizations, especially those supporting LGBTQ+ military as she is an Air Force veteran and Wounded Warrior herself. She can be found on all socials under @misstashadane. *Photo credit: Jerome Simpson*

Temple Grandé

Temple Grandé (she/her/hers), the Squeeze Machine of Brooklyn, is a bearded Queen based in New York City, United States. Originally from the San Francisco Bay Area, Temple Grandé is California girl with a New York zip code. She is a former Chorus Queen of the New York City Gay Men's Chorus (NYCGMC). Hirsute with a body to boot, Temple is a triple threat – she can sing, act, and strip! You heard that right! She's a part-time woman who can tassel twirl with the best of them. She also loves to restyle wigs! You can find her on Instagram @temple_grande. If you need a big, bold body positive DRAG and burlesque star for your next show or a wig that needs some love – email hellotemplegrande@gmail.com for bookings & rates. Temple started her DRAG journey in Spring 2018 and will continue on until Schwarzkopf discontinues Göt2b Glued Hairspray.

Teri Taylor

Teri Taylor is my stage name. In the '70s I used the stage name Twiggy when I was in California at the Queen Mary in Studio City, California, United States. I got my start from my mother, Ronnie Russell, back in Studio City. He said I would be a good performer. I became one at the Queen Mary and won many awards for lip syncing including Miss California and other titles. In the late '60s and early '70s, after leaving California, I went on to become Terry Taylor and continued to perform up until the late '80s due to reasons beyond my control. I gave it up because it was destroying me as a person. I loved performing,

Tessa Martinez

Hello to all, my name is Tessa Martinez. I am a 37-year-old Trans Queen, promoter, emcee, show host, and entertainer born in Oklahoma, United States, living in Hot Springs Arkansas, I celebrated my 20th anniversary in show businesses July 14, 2022. This is one of my most important achievements in my life. I have and traveled near and far to perform, owning my own production company, Stunner Productions, I currently host The GOLD Show and themed nights at Maxine's Live in Hot Springs Arkansas, and a monthly show in Fort Smith, Arkansas at Club Kinkeads. I am so lucky to travel with PussyWillow Productions as well. I have done 1084 performances, 434 Songs, 133 Collaborations so far in my twenty years! I am currently Miss. Twin Cities Elite, promoter of Mr. And Miss. Spa City Pride Pageant! Find me on Facebook, Instagram, and Snapchat.

Thomas A. Eddyson

Thomas A. Eddyson wanted to be a priest, but was considered too salacious for seminary. Instead, he studied film and science and has since put down roots in the Bible Belt, now calling Atlanta, Georgia, United States home. This heavenly hellion's DRAG has been described as "accessible sacrilege" and he's brought audience members to tears with both comedic and sentimental acts. He produces and hosts the bimonthly Sinful Sundays Variety Show at Red Light Cafe in Atlanta. Recently, he performed at the inaugural Hostess City Hoedown Burlesque Festival in Savannah, Georgia alongside burlesque hall-of-famers and has disgraced various stages across the southeastern United States. You can follow Thomas on Instagram at @thomasaeddyson or e-mail at ThomasAEddyson@gmail.com. *Photo Credit: Elegant Life Boudoir*

Thomas Occhio

Thomas Occhio (France) A dandy seducer, who embraces his masculine femininity or is it his feminine masculinity? No matter, he navigates between the genders to better get off the beaten track. Thomas always keeps an eye on you, he likes to observe and be observed. Convinced that everyone wants his body, he offers himself without counting the cost to the public, to you.

Are you a DRAG Performer?
Get on the DRAG411 group on facebook
(not the page) to get your DRAG profile in the
2023 International "Who's Who of DRAG" Directory

Thorne Hart

Thorne Hart is a DRAG King from Hammond, Louisiana, United States. He has been performing all around Louisiana since 2014. He has also competed in the USofA pageant system, recently capturing the title, Mister Louisiana USofA MI. He is known as the metal King, bringing the metal, the sexiness, the laughter and the weird to the stage. He is also a small business owner of Moon Twin Creations, LLC. His dream is to be a full-time artist and performer, vending his wares and performing all over the world. His journey can be followed through Patreon, Instagram, and Facebook.

Tierra Stone

"The Mother of Huntsville" resides in north Alabama. I entered my first talent night in 1991, won and I have been hooked ever since. I am a Trans entertainer, that loves to help others. I enjoy making everyone smile. From ballads to rap, I do enjoy switching up things, especially for the stage. I've hosted many benefit shows, raising money for HIV/AIDS OUTREACH, individuals in need and always looking for ways I can help. I am an activist for LGBTQIA+ community, fighting for equal rights. I want anyone that comes in my presence, to leave feeling better. Be kind to one another. My social media accounts, Facebook TierraStone. TIKTOK @tierrastone42. Instagram Tierra42

Check out the book
Joey Brooks,
The Show Must Go On
From the publisher of DRAG411

Tina Louise

I am trans! When I was seventeen years old, I realized I could entertain and dress as the sex I preferred for a living. I was introduced to the art of Female Impersonators and for fifty years has been my life. "I always wanted to be a star, close enough!" In August 2022 Tina Louise was honored for her fifty years of entertaining in Nashville.

Tishina La Tush

Tishina La Tush and Sunny Daye are the power couple in one body. Hailing from Mi'kma'ki (Halifax, Nova Scotia, Canada); he's a combination gothic emo, geek, kinkster. She is a glittery, magical mess! Throw them together and you have 2020 GenderFuck Supreme Mx winner of the Slay Bells Ball 2020 and the producer and host of Dis-DRAG! a Disney inspired DRAG and burlesque revue. They sing, pretend to dance, and they will introduce you to some amazing mashups (you may or may not hate them for doing it too). Facebook: Tishina La Tush. Instagram: tishinalatush. Tiktok: tishinalatush_sunnydaye. YouTube: Tishina La Tush/Sunny Daye.

Every October we collect the information posted in these books from the DRAG performers. They provide us the information. If someone is missing, it is because they have not sent us their biography and picture... yet. Each book we hope to double in size. This is the first "International Who's Who of DRAG" book.

Tita Titsling

Tita Titsling is Honolulu's Premiere Mustache Queen. Aloha from Honolulu, Hawaii, United States. Tita is a one-of-a-kind entertainer. She began her DRAG seven years ago at a little place called Ong King Art Center. From there she grew her passion and talent through numerous productions. She has hosted the Hawaii Burlesque Festival, The Tropical Fish Show, and DRAG Brunch at Proof. She's outrageous, retro and raunchy. You can find Tita around town hosting shows with all her lovely Honolulu sisters! @TitaTitsling on Instagram, Facebook & Twitter, for booking inquiries: titatitslinghi@gmail.com.

Tobe Danieles

I am Tobe Danieles, a masculine male who is at times a bit of a dork. Weakness for '80s music but spiked and studded rocker is my signature. I've been doing DRAG roughly about eleven years now. I live in Spokane, Washington, United States. First DRAG show was in Moscow, Idaho at a college, all age DRAG show, and decided to try something new. From there, I taught myself to do King make up to look more than a woman dressed in men's clothing. I have picked up some pointers from queens by watching them get ready. I've performed all over Washington, Idaho, Oregon, and Montana. I've created all of my outfits myself and with the assistance of my fiancé of nine years; who is now also a local King. Inspirations to me come from anywhere and anything, most of the time it just pops in my head listening to music. Right now, I hold the title of Prince #46 of the Imperial Sovereign Court of Spokane and we raise money to give back to our community with the art of DRAG. DRAG has saved my life along with many of the people I have met that saved me in one way or another. I keep performing DRAG for the love of it and to further inspire others that they can be and do anything. Instagram and Facebook as Tobe Danieles. Dannielleolds21@yahoo.com email

TomCat Quinn Khrystian

TomCat Quinn Khrystian is a Tulsa, Oklahoma, United States based King who became labeled as the Steampunk King. He is also notorious for his rocker side with an occasional comedy side. The artist behind TomCat has been performing in one way or another since toddler years, but TomCat was born August of 2016. He has held a few titles starting with his first title being a bar title, Prince of Stonewall. His first big pageant won him 1st alternate of Mister Missori UsofA MI Classic 2016, followed by winning the crown in Arkansas the following year as Mister Arkansas USofA MI Classic 2017. TomCat is always working to broaden his craft and has even traveled in surrounding states. The skies the limit. TomCat even has a Diva side by the name of Kitty, making this King quite versatile. Social media: Instagram: king.tomcat.khrystian, Kitty_the_dark. Facebook: Tommy Quinn Khrystian, TomCat Quinn Khrystian (fan page). *Photo Credit: Carrie Strong*

Tommy Boy

Dubbed as the Prince Charming of the Twin Cities, Tommy Boy is your friendly neighborhood DRAG King of Minnesota, United States. I love to create numbers that inspire me to better myself as a person. I love to travel and do lots of different types of shows and I'm always up for a challenge. There are even some crowns on the shelf. Tommy shows the face and confidence onstage that I may not have off-stage in daily life. At the end of the day, Tommy wants to have fun with his fellow performers and the audience!

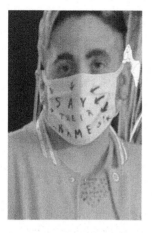

Travis Hard-Monet

I'm Travis Hard-Monet from Milwaukee Wisconsin, United States. I have been doing DRAG thirteen years. I have many bar and state titles to my name. I am lucky enough to have performed on many stages all across the country and hope someday to turn my digital DRAG competition <Apocalypse King, Queen, and Mx> into an in-person pageant system!

Travis Mc'Nasty

Travis is from Cleveland, Ohio, United States. He has been performing since 2006. Though his style has changed a little over the years, his genres have always been eclectic. Known for his particular affinity to be a dirty boy, is often referred to as Daddy. Hip hop; metal; obscure; goth; emo; pop, Travis has many looks and many faces. He loves to freak people out right after he has seduced them. He was part of the (CKG) Cleveland Kings and girls. This is where he got his start. First at a bar called the Grid in Cleveland, Ohio and then later at Bounce Night Club. He currently performs all over Northeast Ohio as well as Akron, Ohio. At the end of the day, he wants to inspire others to be their true self, to be whomever they want to be. Instagram: tmcnasty009

Check out the book
Turn Around Bright Eyes
The Drag Queen Killer
From the publisher of DRAG411

Traynbow

I have been performing since 2006. Being on stage is my passion making people happy through music gives me an adrenaline rush. I have earned a few titles in my performing career. Including Mr. Capital City 2008, Mr. Gay Prom King 2008, Mr. Xcalibur 2009, Mr. Kansas Regional International Inc. 2010, Duke and currently Prince of the Supreme Court 2011, and Mister Black Cosmopolitan International. I am also first alternate to Mr. Black Transman International 2015. I am the current reigning Mr. Black Trans International Kansas 2019 to the present. Music is the only way I feel like I can express myself and people actually understand me.

Trixy Valentine

Trixy Valentine is a DRAG Queen from the North Eastern and Susquehanna Valley Region of Pennsylvania, United States, who uses DRAG as self-expression and advocacy work. I have made community change through many variations of DRAG shows in small conservative towns. I have learned how to have the confidence to stand for others in the community who feel they have no voice. Through such DRAG work, I have increased my platform in my own sex education business at JuicywithJake.com. and became a community leader in starting three local Pride events. My DRAG is beyond the hair, wig, and makeup; it is in the attitude, professionalism, and being a role model for so many. From starting in 2014 to now, I have won titles and created a name, but I have always learned a crown does not make you royalty; it is your commitment to excellence! Photo Credit, Tyler Ryan Studio

V. Beldam

V. Beldam, The Chameleon Creature, the ever-evolving oddball. Changing faces comes naturally to this creature born from the ether. Bringing their signature blend of weird, wild, and sexual theatrics to the stage, with V. Beldam, you never quite know which creature will haunt your dreams. V. is one of the youngest members of the illustrious Haus Contraire. Based along the gulf coast region of the United States, but this beast is primarily found in beautiful New Orleans, Louisiana. Just one question? Are you ready to lose your V. card? Instagram: @V_beldam. Instagram: @hauscontraire.

Vagenesis

Vagenesis is the District of Columbia's black bearded beauty; the tallest, hairiest petite woman in the United States' capital. She started performing in spring of 2018 and has been taking the capital's DRAG scene by storm. She brings a unique brand of comedy and charisma to each of her performances. Vagenesis is an activist, advocating for all styles of DRAG, queer people, and all people of color. She is the creator of Black Label - a showcase of black queer artistry - and promotes inclusive casting and representation in all of her shows. Out of DRAG, they are known as Anderson, a maker of theatre, an acting teacher, and an outspoken non-binary activist for all marginalized groups. Vagenesis was the winner of Cobalt's DRAG Wars season 3, the TikTok DRAG Contest season 1, Captain Green Lantern 2020, and she is the first and current reigning National Bearded Empress. She considers herself first and foremost to be a storyteller and uses every performance opportunity to tell a new tale. Hers is a story you won't want to miss.

Vanessa Rae Peterson

Vanessa Rae Peterson, the Dancing Diva of the Treasure Coast, Port St. Lucie, Florida, United States is a 34-year-old Dominican Capricorn that was born on New Year's Eve. Though DRAG is relatively new to her, she has been a performer for most of her life. Starting shows in the living room for her family to enjoy. Following this passion for performance in kindergarten to 12th grade school, she was awarded a dance scholarship and was able to get a degree in dance and choreography. DRAG was a natural progression of art for Vanessa. She found her passion for the art when she was cast as Chantel in La Cage Aux Folles. Following this interest, she began to attend local DRAG shows in Port Saint Lucie where she choreographed performances for other performers and building shows. It was at that time that she met her DRAG mother, Ashley Peterson. Ashley gave her the guidance needed to follow her heart and dreams. Vanessa continues to perform across the state, named as the Duchess of Port Saint Lucie by the Imperial Sun Court of all Florida. She works with the Imperial Sun Court, a non-profit, to help raise money for good causes. Using her talents to spread love, light, and healing to the world.

Vantasia Divine

Hello all my lovely's, I am the bearded beauty Vantasia Divine from Pensacola, Florida, United States. My DRAG started when I was very young, watching Ru Paul's DRAG Race on television. My mom wanted me to be on that show so bad, but I never saw myself doing it due to social anxiety and self-perception issues. In 2015 when I was fourteen, she unfortunately passed away by her own hand. My world fell into ruin and I never had something to help ease my pain. After a few years of living with my dad, one forced marriage, and another failed marriage, I finally went to college in Massachusetts. I saw my first live

DRAG show at eighteen and immediately wanted to take part of it. Thus, Vantasia was born in December of 2019. After Covid struck, I moved back to Pensacola where I lived with an amazing family who still treat me as their own family. I thought that my DRAG days were over so I started pursuing other goals until I was introduced to a show director here and started my career as a bearded queen. I am one of two bearded queens in Pensacola and use my platform for bearded advocacy, to stand up for equality, to help in the fight against suicidal ideation as well as put on show-stopping performances. This journey has not been the easiest but it's one that I can't wait to include the world in.

Vera DelMar

My name is Richard Barajas, and I am the creator of the DRAG persona known as the Fabulous Vera DelMar, "Tucson's Oldest Living DRAG Queen." I came into DRAG late in life and have been doing it now for seventeen years. I am currently a resident of Tucson, Arizona, United States. My DRAG style is classic DRAG, and total female impersonation. I utilize lip synchronization during my performances. The music I use when I perform can be from the 1960's to now. In my performances I don't do any somersaults, cartwheels, death drops, or any type of gymnastics on stage. I am a "lady" performer after all, and choose to portray one on stage. My favorite artist whose music I enjoy performing to is the late Dusty Springfield. I also enjoy imitating Cher, Tina Turner, and Linda Ronstadt. My repertoire consists mostly of the music of artists like Nancy Sinatra, Bette Midler, Celine Dion, Nancy Wilson, and Reba MacIntire. YouTube or Facebook: Vera DelMar Facebook: richard.barajas (Vera DelMar). Email: lvrosada@hotmail.com *Photo Credit: Jason Castellucci*

It's time to check out
DRAG411.com

Veronica Fox

Veronica Fox, 21 from Indiana, United States. Veronica has been performing since the age of sixteen, and has been a director and emcee of her own shows "The Fox's Den" since the age of 18. She really enjoys entertaining her community and will do anything to help her local Pride board!"

Vicki Vincent

My name is Roget Piatt, my stage name is Vicki Vincent. I began female impersonation in 1981 as a spoof on Halloween. Those that helped me dress, do my hair & makeup were amazed at my transformation. They then challenged me to enter the Miss Gay Missouri Pageant that same year. I did and placed in the top ten on my first attempt. I won the state pageant in 1983. My pageant career had begun. I went on to Miss Gay AMERICA that year and made the top ten as well. I went on to compete and win Miss Four States, Miss Heart of America and Miss Midwest leading up to being crowned Miss Gay America for 1989. I've traveled the country in honor of female impersonation and the rights of all gay people. I've been an avid supporter of the Miss Gay America system and raised hundreds of dollars for HIV/AIDS research and education. I have performed, judged and commentated numerous competitions for nationally recognized organizations as I have been deemed an unbiased and impartial supporter of all pageantry. My personal success in pageantry is due to my Advanced Art awards and my college degree in business management. I've been a Certified Chef for forty years and have cooked for Ted Kennedy, Geraldine Ferrarro, Bob Dole and Patti LaBelle. My home is St. Louis, Missouri, United States. I'm retired from DRAG but still revel in pageantry. I'm one of the blessed people that have survived decades of stage performances. I'm eternally grateful for all the amazing people I've met through my DRAG journey. Being listed in the history books of DRAG is quite humbling and I'm honored to be considered for such an honor. Thank you from the bottom of my heart.

Victoria C. Von Dahlia

My name is Victoria C. Von Dahlia from Hickory, North Carolina, United States. I am a newer bearded Queen doing DRAG for a little over a year. I have one title at a local bar, I am the first Miss Chasers' Bearded Queen 2021. I am the creator and host of my city's first fully alternative DRAG show and pageant known as Freak show. My goals in DRAG are to continue to make waves in the DRAG scene by promoting and supporting alternative DRAG artist. I also plan to compete along "normal" DRAG artist in pageants that are not considered to be for bearded artist. If you are interested in supporting or booking this bearded Queen you can reach out to me through my Facebook page Victoria C. Von Dahlia.

VIKKI SHOKK

An expat from England now living in Florida, United States I publicly came out as a bi gender transvestite and created my alter ego and stage name VIKKI SHOKK in 2019, although I've been secretly dressing as a woman for over 35 years. A repressive religious upbringing and a cultural disapproval of gender non conformity confined me to the closet even though ironically my idol, the iconic English DRAG Queen Danny La Rue was a popular celebrity on mainstream British TV during my formative years. I lost decades of opportunities to be myself because of fear but I'm totally proud of who I am now. Becoming a DRAG Queen is my dream, my way of making up for all those lost years and also a rebellious battle cry against bigotry, prejudice, transphobia and conformity. Ultimately, DRAG isn't just a source of freedom and a means of expression for me... It's a form of REVENGE. I'm looking for opportunities to perform my lip-syncs and a short comedy routine currently in development. I can be found and contacted on social media at the following: Facebook: David Warner (Vikki Shokk) TIKTOK: Vikki Shokk @davidwarner445 INSTAGRAM: @tumbleweed.1965

Viktor Diamond

Viktor Diamond is a 27-year-old non-binary central Kentucky, United States DRAG King whose mission is to spread acceptance, kindness, and love through their art. Viktor passionately spreads information on invisible diseases due to their battle with Ulcerative Colitis. Celebrating one year of DRAG as of May 2022, Viktor has won several titles within Lexington, Kentucky. They frequently perform at Crossings Lexington, The Bar Complex, and several Central Kentucky DRAG brunches. Viktor's background experience in acting, art, cosplay, dance, and makeup has all helped to form the wonderful DRAG persona Central-Kentuckians know and love. DRAG allows Viktor the freedom of self-expression and allows for the utilization of skills acquired throughout many years and disciplines. Viktor strives to bring diversity into the realm of DRAG; they incorporate androgyny, alternative performances, and genderfluidity into their art. Bringing you an electric performance you will never forget, they are Viktor Diamond!

If you search for our books and they say they are "Out of Stock," search again. You are looking at an out-of-print edition. All of the books are in stock, just the older versions are no longer in print (but were re-printed in a newer, available edition).

Viktor Luv Valentine

Viktor Luv Valentine is new to the DRAG scene in Northeast and Central Susquehanna region of Pennsylvania, United States. He is the newest member of the house of Valentine. To be a Valentine means dedication and hard work, to push limits, boundaries and go beyond just the DRAG they do. Viktor Luv is a community leader, volunteer, civic leader, advocate, community activist and DEI Officer (Diversity, Equality, and Inclusion) for the city. "Committed to Community" is his mantra and changing tolerance to acceptance in the community is his mission.

Vinnie Marconi

Vinnie Marconi is still performing at sixty years old. He is best known for comedy numbers and full-on production numbers. Vinnie first hit the stage in 2011 to do a USO benefit and continues to do charity work whenever he is able. He now lives in Clearwater, Florida, United States and has entertained up and down the east coast and parts of the mid-west in the United States. Vinnie has several amateur videos on YouTube and has received local and state pageant crowns. His favorite, however, is representing as Mister St. Pete Pride in 2012 when he was able to give back to the community at different benefits throughout the year. Vinnie's time is spent planning benefits and mentoring male illusionists every step of the way to be the best they can be at the craft. You can follow him on Facebook. She is a lesbian in a long term, loving relationship. My name is Karen, pleasure to meet you! *Photo Credit: Alex Melo*

**Hope you are meeting new entertainers
From around the world of
Different types of DRAG!**

Vintage Blue

Vintage Blue is the new old. This Golden hearted guy is a local DRAG King in Columbus, Ohio, United States who is always down for a good time and for new memories. His style is from punk to old school. Pronouns He/Him/They. Known for being genuine, big hearted, and always making a difference! DRAG King in the (614) and wherever else he wants to go. Give it up for... Vintage Blue. (Area code)

Vivian Darling

She's Rochester, New York's Fat B!tch of DRAG! She being doing DRAG since 2008. She got her start in Allentown, Pennsylvania, United States and now currently resides and works in Rochester, New York. She hosts Roar Nightclub's DRAG Bingo as well as does regular performances. She was first runner up for Miss Gay Rochester 2020. If you want comedy, theatrics, and one-of-a-kind costumes—she's got it. *Photo Credit: Lush Light Photography*

Vivika D'Angelo Steele

It's a pleasure to be featured and share pages with amazing entertainers and ICONS in this industry. Her name is Vivika D'Angelo Steele and is from Tucson, Arizona, United States. Her DRAG mother is Tori Steele and she has thirteen kids; lord these hips need to retire. She is not a dancer but loves to do goofy things along with a great ballad. She wants to show other queens that you don't have to fit in one particular box, DRAG has grown and learning is FUNDAMENTAL. She along with a friend have two monthly shows outside of Tucson

Who's Who of DRAG

and thankful that she has been able to travel to other states to perform and meet many amazing individuals. Has been performing for over ten years and still learning the art of makeup. Love to help our community along with other communities in fundraising.

Warumono

Warumono [he/him]. An international award-winning performer who has been on stage for at least twenty-two years, doing anything from DRAG, burlesque, fire, sideshow, to costuming, acting, music, and events. Originally from Denver, Colorado, United States he now resides in Los Angeles, California. Since moving right before Covid, he finally proudly came out as Intersex and now strives to loudly make sure the 'I' in LGBTQIA+ is not left behind. Yes, Intersex people also do DRAG! Specializing in Cosplay and character acts, as well as what he calls 'Genderfuckery', you never quite know what the expression is going to be, but can be sure he's always a King. Very adamant about pronouns and titles, because who's to say men also cannot have long nails, be feminine, or even tucking and titties? If you're looking to book something fresh and unique, you can find him on Instagram and Facebook @OfficialFilthyWarumono. When not on stage, Warumono is also a loud advocate for normalizing Intersex and other queer/trans bodies in nude spaces, including naturist circles and BDSM communities. All bodies are good bodies no matter their parts. *Photo Credit: Priten Vora*

Are you a DRAG Performer?
Get on the DRAG411 group on facebook
(not the page) to get your DRAG profile in the
2023 International "Who's Who of DRAG" Directory

Whiskey Richards

Smoother than Tennessee whiskey, it's Whiskey Richards! He can be found mainly performing in Mobile, Alabama and Pensacola, Florida, United States. Whiskey got his start in early 2021 after finding a love of doing DRAG while in quarantine. This chivalrous gentleman enjoys expressing different facets of himself on stage. Often channeling a David Bowie or Disney villain vibe, he's not afraid to let his goofy side shine.

Xander Morgan Valentine

Xander Morgan Valentine is a DRAG King with a huge heart and positive energy to match! Xander hails from Central PA and he performs all over the north east. He also co-chairs two Pride committees and donates a majority of his time to community work. Xander's motto: Be kind to yourself, be kind to others, and just be you! *Photo credit Ryan Geiger*

Xavier Bottoms

I am Xavier Bottoms, a 53-year-old DRAG King from Virginia, United States. I have been performing 25 years, since 1997. I have numerous bar titles, many of them I had to compete with cis males. I was the first DRAG King to capture the title of Mr. Capital Pride. I am Mr. Gay United States 2013, my greatest accomplishment. My favorite title in 2007 was Mr. Show Business for the DC Academy of the Performing Arts. I have watched the evolution of DRAG come full circle. I have continuously mentored many DRAG Kings and hope to get a chance to mentor more. My golden rule sim "Don't stop believing in who you are and be real with yourself.

Xavier Diamond

2015 to now. Xavier is your underground overlord in a well-tailored suit. Both a gentleman and a degenerate, he's a father of many DRAG children, and enjoys mentoring as much as performing. Known for his seductive charm and sultry dance moves, people all across North Carolina, United States have been tantalized and teased with a lust for more! Xavier is also very known for hosting events and keeping the crowds laughing throughout the night. You know what they say... Diamond is your girl's best friend. Facebook: Xavier Diamond. Instagram: @xavierdiamonddk. TikTok: @Smol_Yet_Mikki

Xavier Jaxson

Hot Springs, Arkansas, United States. He has been called many things during his eight years on the stage, Mister Little Rock Pride, 1st alt to Mister Arkansas USofA Mi, Mister Spa City Pride, but his favorites are Brother, role model and mentor. Well known for playing on the dark side of the stage, whether it's with his smoking clothes illusion or his disappearing fire trick, he's always finding new ways to keep your eyes on him. He has recently started a traveling DRAG King troupe known as the "Kings of The Springs" doing takeover shows in four different states so far. Photo Credit: Heather Lane, L&L photography

Reach out to these performers;
Tell them where you found them!

Xyvien

Xyvien is a transgender Pittsburgh, Pennsylvania, United States DRAG King that is most known for his ability to paint! His face transforms into a different character to tell a different story every time he performs. Although he has only been performing for about six months, he was born off of his DRAG Queen persona Xyber who has since taken a step down to let Xyvien flourish. Xyvien loves to perform early 2000s emo and rock but isn't afraid to try new genres. He also loves anything flow art! He has incorporated both silk fans and LED poi into performances in the past and doesn't plan to stop any time soon. His main goal is to make people more aware of the amount of talent that both DRAG Kings and trans performers bring to the stage. Xyvien's motto is "wake from dead and return to life like a phoenix"

Zad Gravebone

Zad Gravebone is the undead cartoon King hailing from Boston, Massachusetts, United States. Zad brings you underworld camp and physical comedy. Previously an animator and cartoonist, he started his DRAG debut October 2019 in the King For A Day class taught by Jayden Jamison KA St. James. in 2020, Zad joined the family Stone, headed by Severity Stone, via Zad's DRAG father Travis Tí Stone. DRAG became a new medium for Zad to bring his cartoon persona to life on the live stage. Gravebone's DRAG symbolizes the journey of his transmasculine experience, encapsulating death of an old role and a second chance at life. In June of 2021, Zad went on to win digital DRAG competition "Now Serving", hosted by Violencia Exclamation Point and Majenta with a J. As well as a finalist, as of this writing, in the Boston DRAG Gauntlet. You can find Zad on Instagram @zadgravebone. Photo Credit: Mélis Kooyomjian Kemp

Zaddy D

Zaddy D is the Chocolate Abyss of Kansas City, Missouri, United States. In their first year of DRAG, they have had the opportunity of performing through the big main DRAG venues of Kansas City including Missie B's and Hamburger Mary's. With hips like honey, and a smile that'll melt you to your knees, this King is making it their duty to bring more androgyny to the DRAG King scene.

Zayne "The Dragon" RiAll

Hello everyone. My name is Zayne "The Dragon" RiAll. I am a 38-year-old DRAG King from Central Arkansas. I started DRAG in 2016 when my brother was unable to compete in a pageant, where he had already paid an entry fee. The bar allowed me to use his entry fee in his place and "The Dragon" was born. I have competed in the Classic division of the USofA MI system and in 2018 I was awarded the Brotherhood Award for my support of my brothers and sisters in all things DRAG and in life. DRAG has brought my life so much color and has helped me find a true family whom I love so very much. One thing that can be said about Zayne, is that he never gives up, no matter what obstacles appear or how complicated life gets. He will always remain humble and kind.

Hope you are meeting new entertainers
From around the world of
Different types of DRAG!

Zephyr Shadow

Zephyr Shadow began performing as a DRAG King with the House of Gore in April 2018. Prior to COVID, he performed monthly in Sault Ste. Marie, Michigan, United States, and 3-4 times per year in Sault Ste. Marie, Ontario, Canada. He has recently immigrated from Michigan to Ontario but plans to continue performing on both sides of the international border. Zephyr is the resident "bad boy" of his DRAG family and is often called on to perform lap dances for birthdays and bachelorette parties. Despite his bad boy image, "Zeph" has been referred to as the "heart" of the family and his soft side can be seen when he forgoes a rock/pop number in favor of an upbeat Disney number. Zephyr does his best to record and post all his performances on social media, so be sure to check him out on Facebook or Instagram: Zephyr.Shadow

Every October we collect the information posted in these books from the DRAG performers. They provide us the information. If someone is missing, it is because they have not sent us their biography and picture... yet. Each book we hope to double in size. This is the first "International Who's Who of DRAG" book.

Every year we will post DRAG411's

Official, Original DRAG Memorial
As it is posted on this date on
DRAG411.com

If you go on the site and notice a name missing, simply email me
their name on and off from stage.

We dedicate the International Who's Who of DRAG books to those
entertainers now performing on a grander stage, including these
1564 names: Aalbert Martijn Smit, Aami Dyshea, Aarica Mincey,
Aarica Shane, Aaron Losey, Aaron Von Baron, Abbey Rhoades,
Aboyda Stragg, Ada Buffet, Adam Richards, Adam West, Adam
Winsor, Adeva Blaze, Adoni Bolhar, Adrain (Ada) James, Adrain
Perez, Adrella, Adrian Adair, Adrian Ames, Adrian James Thorpe,
Adrian Lamont, Adrian Sanchez, Adrian Ty'lle, Adrienne Ashe, Africa
Brooks, AJ "Mandi" Millan, Alan Sheenan, Alana Kela, Alanis Casipit,
Alanis Laurell, Alejandro Santana Tavio, Alex C. (Chucky)
Montgomery, Alex Forrest, Alex Hernadez, Alex Soto, Alexa
Whateva, Alexandria Diaz, Alexis Arquette, Alexis Bone't, Alexis
De'Milo, Alexis Fairchild, Alexus, Alice Kooki H. Mizuki, Alina
Hemingway, Alisha Harris, Allan Jarrett, Allan Maloney, Allen Haines
Ramsey, Alotta Whoremones, Alyssa Day, Alyssia Williams, Amancio
Corrales, Amanda from the Freaks, Amanda Love, Amazing Grace,
Amber Clare, Amber Haze, Amber Richards Amber Richards, Amber
Starr, Amii Dyshea, Amy J Jackson, Anastacia Lee, Andre Adore,
Andre Hale, Andrea Nicole, Andy Holmes, Andy Klitty, Andy Lucas,
Angel Chico, Angela Aaron Winchester, Angela Evans, Angelica
Hines, Angie DeMarco, Angie Dickinson, Angie Xtravaganza, Anika
Glam Moore, Anita Thomas, Anthony Jerome Lee, Anthony Lee,
Anthony Luis Laureano Disla, Antoine Ashley, April Eudy Simelane,
April Greer, Arabia Knight-Addams, Arden (Von) York, Areatha
Flowers, Aric Potter, Ariel Andrews, Ariel Maranda Gibbs, Arthur
Caesars, Arturo Galster, Ash Barber, Ashley Adams, Ashley

Alexander, Ashley Ann Summers, Ashley Chambers, Ashley Dior, Ashley Kelly, Ashley Kruiz, Ashley Monroe, Ashley Nason, Ashley Paige, Ashley Summers, Asia Alexander, Aspen Love, Asya Alexander, Aubree Ryan, Audrey Arden, Audrey Morgan, Auntie Flo, Auntie Mame, Aunye Iman Diamond, Authur Wilson, Avis Pendavis Avonte Iman, Barbette, Barbie Grant, Barrie Stevens, Barry Guarino, Barry Lane Hickey, Basia, Bati Star, Becky Boom Boom Bouvier, Beki Goldstein, Belle Kinkade, Benjamin Reid, Benjamin Smoke, Bernard Alan Davidson, Bernie MacDonald, Bert Savoy, Bertha Butts, Beryl Gumm, Bess Anderson, Bette Davis, Beulah Lemont, Beverly LaSalle, Bianca Boujaeu, Bianca Brinski, Bianca Davenport Starr, Bianca DeMonet, Bianca Paige, Big Mama, Big Momma Maybelle, Bill Roy, Billie Blake, Billie Boots, Billie Dodson, Billy "Mother" Boots, Billy Piper, Bliss Blaisedale, Blossom O'Toole, Bob Bombara, Bob Gale, Bobbie Callicoate, Bobbie Holiday, Bobbie Janson, Bobby Compian, Bobby Crane, Bobby DeCastro, Bobby Etienne, Bobby Marchan, Bobo O'Neal, Boi George, Boom Boom LaTour, Bothwell Browne, Brad Hall, Brandi Houston, Brandi McDaniels, Brandy Alexander, Brandy Dover, Brazon, Breezy St. James, Brenda Blake, Brenda Dale Knox, Brenda Dee, Brenda Lee, Breneisha, Brent Moreland, Bri Alexander, Brian Benton, Brian Clark, Brian Fox, Brianna Colby, Britany Fairchild, British Sterling, Brittany Brandfas, Brittney Wells, Bruce Falls, Bruce Williams, Buffy Demaro, Buhlah LaMonte, Bunny Lane, Bunny Lewis, Burmon King, Busty Ross, Butchie Tanner, Byron Coleman, Cameron B. Tanner, Candi Cabrini, Candi Wilson, Candice Carrington, Candice Kelly, Candie Van Cartier, Candy Booth, Candy Du Barry, Candy Dubarry, Candy Wills duBarry, Cari Wayne, Carl Rizzi, Carlotta, Carmel Santiago, Carmella Marcella Garcia (Mella), Carmen Del Rio, Carmen Rupe, Carmen, Carole Jackson, Carolyn Frye, Carrie Dennis, Carrie Phillips, Casey Cole, Cashetta, Cassandra Blake, Cassandra Gay, Cassandra Mills-Best, Catrina Avilon, CC Lines, Cece Deval, CeCe LaCroix, Cedric Patton, Celine Crawford, Champagne Howell, Champale Denise, Chanaile Solitaire, Chanel Devine Sherrington, Chanel St. James, Chanel White, Chante Seville, Chantel McKee, Chantelle Douglas, Chardonnay Le Tease, Charlene Rose, Charles Aaron Grimes Winchester, Charles Ludlam, Charles McDuff Gillis, Charles Parr, Charles Pierce, Charlie Brown, Charlie

Davis, Charlotte Parr, Charlotte, Chelsea Pearl, Chelsea Shanese, Chena Kelly, Cherelle Ventura, Cherine Alexander, Cherry Cola, Chi Chi DeVayne, Chi Chi Laverne, China Doll, Chip Thomas, Chivonne Street   Chloe Coleman, Chocolate Monague, Chocolate Thunderpussy, Chris Ames, Chris Culligan, Chris Edwards, Chris Morgan, Chris Scheff, Chrissie, Christi Cole, Christian Paige, Christie Cole, Christie Lane, Christopher van Pelt, Chuck Atteberry,, Chyna Doll Dupree, Chyna Gibson, Cicely Berlin, Ciji Michaels, Cinnamon, Cissy Goldberg, Cladette Knight, Claire Sheradin, Clarissa Cavalier, Claudette Night, Claudio G. Lake, Clay Edwin Lambert, Clay Hester, Clayton Hamilton, Clif E Waters, Clifford Vicks, Cloe Coleman, Coco, Codie Leone, Codie Ravioli, Cody McGuire, Cole Walker, Colin Devereaux, Coma, Connell Howell, Connie Carlylse, Connie Dupree, Connie Marcell, Constance Calcutta, Constance Monroe, Cookie Dough, Cookie LaCook, Cookie McCoo Childress, Corwin Anthony Hawkins, Cory Good, Cote' Rossmore, CP, Craig Loucks, Craig R. Eadie, Craig Russell, Crave Moorehead, Cruella Divine, Crystal Blue, Crystal Clear, Crystal DeVille, Crystal Starr, Crystal, Cynde Page, Daddy K, Daisy Dalton   Daisy Dube, Daisy Dynamite, Dakota Carmichael, Dale Barnette, Dale Johnson, Dalila, Dame Glenda, Dame Hilda Bracket, Damien McClinton, Dan Bisson, Dan Curry, Dana Manchester, Danee Russo Rodriquez, Dani Daletto, Daniel Booth, Daniel Crystal, Daniel D. Perry, Daniel Davis, Daniel Flier, Daniel Patrick Carroll, Dannielle Crystal, Danny Billington, Danny Day, Danny Hurshman, Danny King, Danny LaRue, Danny Leonard, Danny Love, Danny Windsor, Dante Brown, Danyelle Winters, Daphne Delight, Daphne Devore, Daphne Prideaux, Daray Lorez, Darin Shane Honeycutt, Darla Childs, Darla Delicious, Darlene Duncan, Darnell K., Darrell Myers, Darren West, Dave Pollard, David Cain, David Desire, David Feldstein, David John Wayne MacDonald, Davina Delmar, Deborah Debt, Dede Divore, Dee Dee Lewis, Dee Dee Williams, Deja Knight, Deliah O'Neal, Della Reeves, Demetrios "Jimmy" Karahalios, Dena Malloy, Dena Michaels, Denise Darshell, Denise Fairchild   Denise Michaels, Dennis VanBelle, Derek Hood, Derrick Smith, DeShawna Hughes, Desiree De'Marco, Desiree Love, Destiny Foster, Destiny Rae   Deva Sanchez, Devine, Dexter Colston, Diamond Lil, Diamonds Lamour, Diana Black, Diana Hutton, Diana

Stryker, Diane Jackson, Diane Torr, Dianna Hubbard, Dick Peltz, Didi Jagger, Didi Piaf, Dion (Martel) Martell, Dior Dandridge, Dirt Woman, Divine, Dixie Crystals, Dixie D. Cupp, Dockyard Doris, Dolly Love, Dominique Sanchez, Domino D-lite, Don Flowers Randolph, Don Middlemiss, Don Seymour McLean, Donald E. Smith, Donald George Shelton, Donald W. Davis, Donna Day, Donna Drag, Donni DuPont, Donnie Corker, Dorian Corey Dorian Wayne, Doris Fish, Dottie West, Doug Austen, Dougie Anderson, Dreama Andrews, Dreama St. Love, Drew Mancuso, Duncan Do Not, Dusti Hymen, Dusty Deville, Dusty Diamond, Dutchess von Wick, Dyan Michaels, Dyanna Stryker, Dyiamond Dynasty, Eartha Quake, Ebony Hall, Ebony, Ed Wood, Eddie Bell, Edie Holiday, Edward Davis "Ed" Wood Jr., Edward Knepp, Edward Smith, Edye Goldsby, Edye Gregory, Elaine St. Jaques, Ellen Diamond, Elsa Maxwell, Endora Van Cartier Clinton, Enrique Hinojosa Vázquez, Epiphanie, Eric Farrow, Erica Adams, Erica Andrews, Erica Lane, Erica Lucci, Erica Meadows, Erica Renee Knight, Erica Shane, Erica Sommers, Erica Van Cort, Erik Johnston, Erik Knight, Erika Mills, Esteban Romero, Ethel Bailey, Ethyl Eichelberger, Eva Destruction, Evan St. John, Eve Starr, Evelyn Davis, Evelyn Sanchez, Fabiola, Faith Iman, Fantasy Starr, Farrah Amanda McCray, Felicia Adams, Felicia Blackhart, Felicia Gallant, Felicia Mark, Felicia Mortuiccio, Felicia Winters, Felitia Fahr, Felton Day, Feral Beral, Fernando Gomez, Flawless Sabrina, Flo Floé, Fonda C. Lord, Foo Foo (Lamarr) Lammar, Fran Jeffries, Francis Leon, Francis Patrick Glassey, Francis Renault, Francis Russell, Frank Adair, Frank Devera Jackson, Frank Doran, Frank Lamarr, Frank Pearson, Frankie Barry, Frankie Jaxon, Fred Cotton, Jr., Fred Cougan, Freddy Cortez, Freddy Renault, Frieda Lay, Fritz Capone, Gabrielle "Gabby" Berlyn, Gabrielle Sizemore, Garfield West, Gary Gagnon, Gary Mangum, Gary McMurtry, Gary Mullins, Gayla Mccord Delust, Gayle Lynn, Gemini, Gene La Marr, Gene Malin, George Peduzzi, George Timothy Reed, Georgia Brown, Gerald J Mayes, Gerard George Andrews, Geri Day, Gib Hauersperger, Gigi Mayonae, Gigi, Gilbert Baker, Gina De Anton, Ginette Bobo, Ginger Grant, Ginger Lamar, Ginger Manchester, Ginger Monroe, Ginger Nichole, Ginger Spice, Ginger Taylor, Ginger Vitus, Gita Gilmore, Glam Moore, Glen Paulin, GlenGlen Wagner, Grand Prix, Grande, Great Scagnolia,Greg Green,

Gregory Cohn, Gregory Courtesis, Guilda, Guy Carroll, Hal Wadell, Hank Lintjer, Hans van den Hoek, Harold Waller, Harris Glenn Milstead, Harry Hodges, Harry S. Franklyn, Harvey Lee, Heather Anton, Heather D'Haven, Heather Hunter, Heavy Duty, Heavy Metal, Helena Hologram, Henry Boyd, Hillary Matthews, Hollie Wood, Holly Brown, Holly Daze Crystals, Holly St. Clair, Holly Woodlawn, Hope Holloway, Howard Meyer, Howard Shortsleeve, Howard Tipler, Hunter Smith, Ida Nurse, Ignacio Rodriguez, Ima Twat, Image Devereux, Imani Tate, Imogene Wilson, Indigo Luvsumme Blue, Irving Ale, Isabella Frost, Issan Dorsey, Issy St. James Escada, Ivana / Ivanna, Ivonna Hump, Ivory Díor, Ivy White, Jack Doroshow, Jack Roberts, Jackie Knight Jackie Roberts, Jackie Wilson, Jacqueline Pissybottom, Jae Stevens, Jagger Blue, Jahnau Reis, Jalissa Aundrea Michaels, James Arthur Fuller, James Carroll, James Clark, James Crews, James Demas, James Harrington, James Levi, James McDowell, James Pascoe, James Roy Eichelberger, James St. James, James Thorpe, Jamie Carroll, Jamie Christian, Jamie Levi, Jamie Silver, Jan Chamblee, Jan Howard, Jan Payne, Jana Steele, Jarmon Mayes, Jasmine Knight, Jasmine Perry, Jason Bradley, Jason Lincoln, Jason-Ivy White, Javon Phelps, Jay Monro, Jay Russel, Jayda Beyonce Taylor, Jazz, Jean Guida de Mortellaro, Jean Malin, Jeanetta Williams Jeanie "Tits" Duval, Jeff Gibson, Jeff Johnson, Jeff Miller, Jeff Tagg, Jeffrey Lithcum, Jemma Storm, Jennifer Harlow, Jennifer Holliday Chanel, Jennifer Lakes, Jennifer North, Jennifer Raquel, Jennifer Welles, Jenny McCall, Jere Williams, Jeremi Morris, Jeremy Greer, Jerri Daye, Jerry Clanton, Jerry Luna-Rockwell, Jesse Scott, Jessenia Marie Rosa, Jessica Jackson, Jessica Jazz Ross, Jessica Nolan, Jill Jordan, Jill-Ette Knicks, Jim Bailey, Jim Fancil, Jim Peterson, Jimi Dee, Jimmie Dee, Jimmy Clem, Jimmy Dillard, Jimmy McCollough, Jimmy Smith, JoAnn Delite, Jocelyn Anthony, Joe Cline, Joe Collins, Joe Jackson, Joel Castillo, Johanna Steel, John Anthony Gonzales, John Atkinson, John Barber, John Byrne, John Cely, John Gonzales, John Goodman, John Goodwin, John Harvey, John Lonas, John Martin, John Palmer, John Schaefe, John Zarrelli, Johnelle Vincent, Johnny Maddox, JoJo, Jolie London, Jomy Cyriac Abraham Theradiyel, Jordan Alexander, Jordan Blake, Jose Jimenez, José Julio Sarria, José Rigual, Joseph Stevens, Josh Hamburg, Joshua Horton,

Josie Desmond, Juan M Estrada, Judy Judy, Julian Eltinge, Junior Larkin, Justin Flowers, K.C. Carrington, Kaitlyn Cain Kandy Johnson, Kara Dion, Karl Williams, Karlita, Karyl Norman, Kate Marlow, Katrina Avalon, Katrina Gail Phillips, Katrina Meeks, Kay Mullinax, Kelley, Kelli Randall, Kelli Randell, Kelly Dagen Kelly King, Kelly Michaels, Kelly Summers, Kelvin Bradley Watkins, Kendra Monroe, Keni Marlo, Kenneth Marlow, Kenneth Melo, Kenneth Poole, Kenny Dash, Kenny Kerr, Kenny Leda, Kenny Whitehead, Keosha Necole "Keke"Cassadine, Kerri O'Kee, Ketty Teanga, Kevin Bauer, Kevin Dorsey, Kevin Rodriquez, Kevin Vaughan, Kiára, Kiarra Cartier Fontaine, KiArra Fontaine Marlowe, Kiarra St. James, Kiki DeCarlo, Kiki, Kiki, Mother, Kim Alexis, Kim Ross, Kim Valdez, Kim, Connors, Kimberly "KJ" Morris, Kirby Kincade, Kitten Do Claw, Kitty Collins, Kitty DeLove, Kitty Litter, Klitty Liqour, Kolby Kincaid, Kristina Grant Infiniti, Kristina Grant, Kristy Love, Krystal Blackhart Knights, Krystal Kelly, Krystal Stone, Kyle Dennis Souder, Kylie O'Reilly La Twig Darling, Lady Ashley Adams, Lady Barbara, Lady Baroness Maria Andrea del Santiago, Lady Cateria, Lady Catira, Lady Chablis, Lady Charisse, Lady Charles, Lady Charlotte, Lady D, Lady Diana, Lady Ebony Hall, Lady Gayle, Lady Geneva, Lady Godiva, Lady Helena Sacowitz, Lady Katiria, Lady Nova Bernard, Lady Pearl, Lady Shawn, Lady Vic, Lady Wincey, Lana Kuntz, Larista Colby, Larry Fox, Larry Huggins, Larry Kidd, Larry Love, Lateasha Shante Shuntel, Latese Chevron, LaTorsha Zannel, Latoya St. James Laura Beth, Laura Lee Love, Lauren LaMasters, Lauren Sugarbaker, Lauryn Paige Fuller, LaVern Banadese Laverne Cummings, Laviita Allen, Lawren LaMoore, Lawrence LaMoore, Lee Paris, Lee Stevens, Leif Roschberg, Leigh Bowery, Lena London, Lennie LaToke, Leo Hernandez, Leonard Kelly, Leonardo Martinez, Leslie Rage, Leslie Rajanne, Leslie Ryan, Leslie Woods, Lester Childress, Lestra La Monte, Letha Weapons, Lexie Love, Libertee Belle, Liesa Durrant, Lilian Carré, Lillian Ross, Lily White, Linda Day, Linda Robinson, Lindsey Love, Liquor Campbell, Lisa Fontaine, Lisa King, Logan Carter, Lola Lush, Lona LaMore Lonnie McElwain, Lori Shannon, Lotta Nerve, Lovely Greta Girl, Lulu LaRude, Lupi Longoria, Luther Nelson Jr., Lyndell Honeycutt, Maddox Madison, Mag Reiley, Maggie London, Maggie Scott, Magnolia Thunderpussy, Mahogany Reason,

Mahogany, Maja Douglas, Malcom Michaels Jr., Malissa Starr, Mallessa Starr, Mama, Mame Dennis, Manzell Avant, Marc Beuter, Marc Fleming, Marcy Marcell, Margo Howard-Howard, Margo, Maria DelMonte, Maria Mendez, Marilyn Chambers, Mario Bermudez, Mark Fleming, Mark Irish, Mark Middleton, Mark William Irish, Marnie, Mars, Marsha P. Johnson, Marty McClain, Mary Kaye, Marylin Lee, Matthew Bogseth, Matthew Burk, Maurice Carter, Maxi Houston, Maxi, Maxine Allen, Maxwell Ritchie, Maya M. Moore, Meela Richardson, Melba Moore, Melba Moore, Melissa D'Moore, Mellisa Blake, Melvin Leachman, Memory Lane, Memphis Deville Richards, Mena Darnell, Mercedes Demarco, Mercedes Denishayae Taylor, Mercedes Gallant, Mercedes Successful, Merlin D "Tommy" Thompson, Merph/Murph Griffin, Merphy Griffin, Meshallay Crystal, Mia Landon, Michael Andrews, Michael Androlewicz, Michael Canterbury, Michael Clarke, Michael Halftery Rater, Michael Leonard Williams, KSG, Michael Murphy, Michael Skaggs, Michael St Laurent, Michael Swayze, Michelle Christina Jones, Michelle Le'More, Michelle Liemont, Michelle Marie, Michelle Ross, Michelle Scott Michelle St James, Michelle St. John, Mickey Day, Mickey LaRue, Mickie Knight, Midnight Annie, Mike Cain, Milla, Millena Hideaway D -Lite, Milton Berle, Mishon Black, Miss Chifon, Miss DeJa Vous Miss Demeanor, Miss Ebony, Miss Flowers, Miss G., Miss Kitty, Miss Mann, Miss Marcus, Miss Markus, Miss Opal Foxx, Miss Opal, Miss P., Miss Petra Fyde, Miss Sammy, Miss Tracy, Miss Understood. Miss Vogue, Miss Whitney, Miss Woochie, Miss-ter Billie Pet Clarke, Misty Knight, Misty McCall, Mitch Bartlett, Mizz Ginger, Moldavia Ishtar, Molly Redmond, Mona Desmond, Mona Foot, Mona Leather, Monica Marlo, Monica Rey, Monica van Pelt,Monique L'Amor, Monique Moore, Morgan Courday, Morgan Courtnay Deveraux, Morgan Farrah, Morgan St. Clair, Morgan Wood, Morrie Carter, Morticia DeVille, Mother Detroit, Mr. Bunny Lewis, Mr. Chip Thomas, Mr. Crystal, Mr. Della Reeves, Mr. Sandy Howard, Mr. Terry Durham, Mr. Tiffany Jones, Mrs. Shufflewick, Ms. Dee, Ms. Marcus, Mya Mokka Iman, Myla Larue, Myrna Vonn, Mysti Dawn, Naiomy Kane, Naomi Sims, Nashom Wooden, Natalie Gaye LaShore, Natalie Greer, Natasha Edwards, Natasha Fields, Natasha Hall, Natasha Richards, Nazhoni T.

Foxx, Neal Horvatits, Neal O'Hara, Neal Scott, Neely O'Hara, Netasha Edwards, Nia Gabrielle, Nichelle Nichols, Nick Connor, Nicki Gallucci, Nicky Young, Nicole Lynn Foxx, Nikki Fenmore, Nikki LeParks, Nikki Silvers, Nikki Starr, Nikki Young Blackpool, Nina Monroe, Nina Rage, Noel Dougherty, Nomi De'Vereaux, Norris Benefield Obvious Heights, Octavia St. Laurent, Odyssey Olivia Pantene, Opal Fox, Owen Pride Roach, Paal Roschberg, Pacifica Rim, Paddy Kakes, Paige Turner, Paivi Lee Love, Paris Chanel, Paris Dupree, Patricia Murphy, Patrick Callahan, Patrick Fyffe, Patrick McGuire, Patrick Murphy, Patrina Marie, Patsy Vidalia, Patti Cakes, Patty Kakes, Paul Ashford, Paulettea Leigh, Pauline St. James, Peach Melba, Peaches La Fleur, Peaches La Pitt, Peg A Go-Go, Peg, Penelope Poupé, Penelope, Pepper LaBeija, Peter Fernandez, Peter Searle, Petrina Marie, Phatima Rude, Phil Starr, Philip Mills, Phillip Forrester, Phillip Rhoads, Phyllis Trammell Poison, Porscha Mercadez, Prdra Austell Hall, Prince D Andrews, Princess Janae Banks, Prissy Divine, Prudence, Pussy Willow, Quinton Crisp, R.C. Cola, R.V. Beaumont, Rachael Leigh, Rachael Masters, Rachaell Santoni, Rachel Winters, RaChelle Wilson, Racine Scott, Rae Bourbon, Raghenna, Raine Scott, Ramona Baker, Ramona LeGer, Ramona Ravenski, Randy Cole, Randy Kelly, Rascal Bottoms, Ray Francis, Raymond Fetcho, RD Walls, Reg Bundy, Regina Fong, Regina Simms, Reginald Finley, Reginald Sutherland Bundy, Reina Valentino, Rene Russo, Rene Van Hulle, Renée Scott, Renee Williams, Reuben Bressler, Reviala Donroe, Rex Jameson, Rhonda Armstrong, Rhonda Leigh, Rhonda Moore, Rhonda Starr, Ric DiMario, Rica Beba, Ricardo Ignacio Zapata, Ricci Russeaux, Richard Greer, Richard Hall, Richard Henson, Richard Hoffman, Richard Masterson, Richard Nichols, Richard Palsgrove, Richard Reese, Richard Thomas, Richard Webb, Ricky Carter, Ricky Cordova, Ricky Glass, Ricky Renee, Rikki Lee, Rikki Summers, Roada Kihl, Robbie Walker, Robert Booth, Robert Dusek, Robert H. Hall, Robert Hesse, Robert Logan Carter, Robert Mitchel-Blough, Robert Penninger, Robert Robinson, Robert Timbrell, Robert Wanke, Robin Banks, Robin Morgan, Robin Wayne, Roby Landers Robyn Hunter, Roger Godfrey, Romona Lager, Ronald Davis, Ronald Dennison, Ronald Jerome Alford, Ronald Norman Simoneau Jr., Rondretta Billingsly,

Ronica Reed, Ronnie McDaniel, Ronnie Reed, Ronnie Russell, Rosa Lake, Rosalyn Delight, Rose Leaf, Rose Marie, Rose Petal, Roshawn Greer, Rosheda Tyia, Rosie Marie, Roski Fernandez, Roslyn Heights, Ross Higham, Roxanne Cordova, Roxanne O'Neil, Roxanne Russell, Roxanne The Latin Lovely. Roxanne, Roxie Cotton, Roxy Marquis, Roy L Derryberry, Roy Steel, Royal Knight, Ruby Dee, Ruby Flame, Rudi D'Angelo, Rudi Rogelio, Rudy de La Mor, Rudy L. Hendrickson, Russell Craig Eadie, Rusty Ryan, Ruud Swanen, RV Beaumont, Ryan Zinc, Ryk McDow, Sabel D' Zyre, Sable Alexander/ Sable Champion, Sable Starr, Sabre Patton, Sabrina Kay Marshall, Sabrina Morgan, Sache VanCartier, Sadie Brooks, Safari Habiel, Sahara Davenport, Sally Mae Sasquatch, Sam Singhaus, Samantha Cleavage, Samantha Love, Samantha, Sammy Duddy, Sammy Thomas, Samuel Collins, Sandee, Sandi Lovelace, Sandra Hush, Sandra Hush, Sandra Playgirl, Sandy Cher, Sandy Howard, Sandy K. Daniels, Sandy Welles Santana T. Summers, Sasha Kennedy, Sasha Loren, Sasha Nicole, Sasha Sommers, Sasha Valentino, Sassie Saltimboca, Satan Deville, Satara Shatin, Satin Rose, Satin Styles, Satryana Blaque, Satyn DeVille, Savannah Kohl, Savion Simpson Black, Savona Campbell, Scabola, Scarlett Fever, Scott Andrew, Scott Weston, Selena Daniels, Sensuous, Serena Hunter, Sha'day Halston-St James, Shafonda Vaughn, Shahgopal Whybrow, Shakira Stevenz, Shan Covington, Shana Steele, Shanell Solitaire, Shangay Lily, Shanice Starr, Shannon Forrester, Sharon Needles, Shavon Marlon Shawn, Shayla Masters, Shayla Simpson, Sheena Angelica, Sheila T. Bailey, Shelita Golden, Shelly Stout, Sheree Franklin, Shereen Dennis, Sheri Powers, Shirleena, Shirley Steel, Shirley Wood, Shirley, Sicely Manchester, Sidney Headburg, Sierra Montana, Sierrah Foxx, Sinclair, Sissy Collins, Sister Roma, Skip Arnold, Sofonda L. Peters, South Beach Wanda, Sovereign Rey'al, Stacey Brown, Stacey Lauren Stacia Leron, Stacy Carlson, Stacy Farrare, Star Montrice Love, Starr LaSalle, Stasha Iman, Stazia, Stella Show Icmeler, Steph Sparkles, Stephani Stamos, Stephanie Blake, Stephanie Bofill, Stephanie Powers, Stephany "Sticky" Daniels, Stephen Cann, Stephen L. Jones, Steve Boeger, Steve Jones, Steven Dale Renner, Steven Gelley, Steven Magyarics, Steven Michael Egan, Steven Nelson, Steven Teets, Steven Yablonski, Stevie Stevens, Stormé DeLarverie

Strawbella Be'AGoddess, Studio X Lenoir, Sultanna Corangie, Summer Holiday, Sweet Savage, Sweetie, Sybil Ann Storm Sybil Santiago, Sybil Smith, Sylvester James, Jr., Sylvester, Sylvia Sidney, Synoman, T. C. Jones, Tabitha Stevens, Tabitha Versace Starr, Tahtiana Kresha, Tajma Hall, Tallulah Banks, Tallulah, Tam Taylor, Tamara Demore, Tamara Fox, Tami DeLove, Tammy Pax, Tandi Andrews, Tandi Dupree, Tandi Iman Dupree, Tanisha Cassadine, Tanisha Caston, Tara Dion, Tara Richmond, Tara Schenelle Starr, Tara-Ash Barber, Tasha Diane, Tatiannah Kreshe, Tawdri Hipburn, Tawnya Toosieroll, Taylor Hill, Ted Larson, Teddy Pedigree Paul, Teighlor Artesk, Temple, Teri Courtney, Teri Jean Arnell, Terri Livingston, Terri Michaels, Terri Rodgers, Terri Rogers, Terri-Jean Arnell, Terry Cummings, Terry Durham, Terry Gardner, Terry Jean Arnell, Terry Knight, Terry La Tour, Terry Livingston, Terry Matthews,, Terry Parnell, Terry Phillips, Terry Pittman, Terry St. Claire, Terry Taylor, TeTe Torez, The Diva Perry, The Lady Chablis, The Tigress, The Widow Norton, Thomas Craig "T. C." Jones, Thomas Fairmakes, Thomas Lincon, Tifani St Jon, Tiffani Jones, Tiffany Daniels, Tiffany Jones, Tiffany Middlesexx, Tiffany Rose, Tiffany Scott, Tiger Lil', Tillie Plumkin, Tim Gillan, Tim Greeley, Tim Moore, Tim Wallace, Timi Tremaine, Timothy Liupakka, Timothy Patterson, Timothy Swain, Tina Braxton, Tina Devore, Tina Renee, Tina Roberts, Tina Schumacher, Tina Templeton, Tina Wells, Tiny Tina, Tionne, Tippi Walker, Tippy Hedron, Tippy, Tish Tanner, Tissy Malone, Toby Marsh, Todd Estes, Todd Shelf, Todd Storti, Tom Yaegy, Tommy Dee, Tommy Dorsey, Jr., Tommy McGuire, Toni Duran, Toni Lenoir, Toni Lenore, Tony Bua, Tony Rose, Tony Russell, Tony Sinclair, Tonya Gayle, Tonya Marie Richardson, Tonya Mullins, Torchie Taylor, Torchy Lane, Torrance Cheeves, Torre Adore, Totie Martel, Trace McNutt, Tracey Lee, Tracey Nichols, Tracey Stephens, Tracey Stevens Tracy "Liz" Adams, Tracy Adams, Tracy Fontain, Tracy Lee, Tracy Morgan, Tracy Savage, Tranny Robert, Trauma Flintstone, Travis Gore, Travis Mark Michael Greenfield, Treasure Gardener, Treva Perry, Treva Trash, Trevor Rupe, Tricksie Turner, Trinity Scott Mathews, Trisha Trash, Trixie Daily, Trixie Taylor, Troy James "Dusty" Lansdown, Troy Williams, Truley LeFemme, Truman May, TT Thompson, Tu Real, Tuna Starr, Tweeka Weed, Twiggy, Tyese Rainz,

Tyler Wicihowski, Tyra Bishop, Ursula Black, Valencia Rollins, Vander Clyde, Vanessa Dell Rio, Vanessa LaSalle, Vanessa Michelle, Vanessa Richards, Vanessa Vanover Vermont, Vanessa Vincent, Vanilla Lush, Vanity Munroe, Vanity Starr, Vaunda Lee, Vaunessa Vale, Venessa Jackson, Venus Alexis, Venus Xtravaganza, Veronica Devore, Veronica Grey, Veronica Lake, Veronica York, Vicci Laine, Vicki Lawrence, Vicki Marlane, Vicki Martin, Vicki Rene, Vickii Vox, Vicky Mandrell, Victor Guimarães, Victoria Burton, Victoria Lamarr, Victoria Sinclair, Victoria St. James, Victoria Towers, Vidas de Herejes, Vincent Hill, Vinny Lick Her Snatch, Vivienne Fontana St. James, Vonda Delaine, Vonda Lee, Vonda Richards, Vonna Valentino, Walter Bell, Walter Dempster, Jr., Walter Flemming, Walter Hart, Walterina Markova, Wanda Lust, Warren Wilson, Waylon Flowers, Wayne Lee Killough, Jr, Wayne Smart, Wesley Aurick McArthur, Wesley Byers, Whitney Jackson, Whitney Paige, William Albert Castellano, William Brett Basher, William Jackson, William Julian Dalton, William L Dodson, Willie Ninja, Yazmina Couture, Yazmine Demornay, Yoyo Fizzure, Yuri Montecarlo, Zack Dejong, Zackary Allen Hubble, Zackary Roberts, Zavion Michael Davenport, Zena Kay Diamonte, Zena Kay, Zsa Zsa D'laHor, Zsa Zsa Principle, and Zuleyka Noir.

Ten Black Books of DRAG411.com
Are now Twelve books!

Book 1   DRAG411's
"DRAG Bully, A Survivor's Guide"

The Largest Bullying Project in LGBT History for Struggling Entertainers. Advice from over a hundred male, female, and androgynous impersonators around the world to help entertainers struggling with their family, peers, relationships, neighbors, regular jobs, venues, and successfully overcoming self-doubt. Best Selling author Todd Kachinski Kottmeier created DRAG411 to document the lives of male, female, and androgynous impersonator years ago. It is now the largest organization for impersonators on earth with over 7,000 entertainers in 32 countries. DRAG411 also operates The International Original, Official DRAG Memorial with almost two thousand names (2022). This is his 25th book, 20th World Record, and 10th book on this subject. Thousands of invitations to contribute were send out. This book contains the best of their responses, in their own words, to you.

Book 2 DRAG411's
"Original, Official DRAG Handbook"

Over 155 female impersonators (and 1 male impersonator) from around the world share over a thousand insightful comments in the first handbook created of this artform.

Commentary shared with Todd Kachinski Kottmeier included the following contributors of The Original, DRAG Handbook to include Ada Buffet, Adora , Adrian Leigh, Afeelya Bunz, Alisa Summers, Alanna Divine, Alexis De La Mer, Alexis Mateo, Alex Serpa, Allure, Amanda Bone, Amanda Love, Amy DeMilo, Anastaia Fallon, Astasnaia Rexia, Angel gLamar, Angela Dodd, Anita Cox, April Fresh, Ashleigh Cooley, Aurora Sexton, Babette Schwartz, Bailey St. James, Barbra Herr, Barbra Seville, Beverly LaSalle, BJ Stephens, Blair Michaels, Brandon M. Caten, Brianna Lee, Brittany Moore, Brookyln Bisette, Bukkake Blaque London St. James, Cartier Paris, Cathy Craig, Champagne T. Bordeaux, Cherry Darling, Christina Paris, CoCo LaBelle, CoCo Montrese, CoCo St. James, Conundrum, Crystal Belle, Daniel Murphy, Danika Fierce, Daphne Ferraro, Dasha Nicole, Dee Gregory, Deva DaVyne, Diamond Dunhill, Diedra Windsor Walker, Dmentia Divinyl/Eva LaDeva, Echo Dazz, Esme Russell, Estelle Rivers, Eunyce Raye, Felica Fox, Felina Cashmere, Geraldine Queen Cabaret, Ginger Minj, Glitz Glam, Gilda Golden, Horchata, Ima Twat, Ineeda Twat, Jade Daniels, Jade Jolie, Jade Shanell, Jade Sotomayo, Jaeda Fuentes, Jami Micheals, Jay Santana, Jeffrey Powell, Jenna Chambers Tisdale, Jessica Jade, Jocelyn Summers, Jodie Holliday, Joey Brooks, Joshua Myers, J.P. Patrick, Juwanna Jackson, Kamden Wells, Katrina Starr, Kenny

Braverman, Khrystal Leight, Kier Sarkesian, Kiki LaFlare Santangilo, Kitty D'Meaner, Kori Stevens, Krystal Amore Adonis, Lacey Lynn Taylors, Lady Clover Honey, Lady Sabrina, Lady TaJma Hall, Lakeisha Pryce, LeeAnna Love, Leigh Shannon, Lisa Carr, Lola Honey, Madisyn De La Mer, Makayla Rose Devine, Maxine Padlock (Maxi Pad), Melissa Morgan, Melody Mayheim, Michael Wilson, Mike Astermon-Glidden, Mis Sadistic, Miss Conception, Miss Gigi, Mr. Kenneth Blake, Misty Eyez, Monique Michaels, Myah Monroe, Mystique Summers, Nairobi V. D'Viante, Naomi D-Lish, Naomi Wynters, Nicole Paige Brooks, Nikki Dynamite, Nova Starr, Ororo, Patrica Grand, Patricia Knight, Patrica Mason, Pandora DeStrange, Penelope Reigns, Polly FunkChanel, Phiore Star Liemont, Purrzsa Kyttyn, Pussy LeHoot, Raquel Payne, Rhyana Vorhman, Rickie Lee, Rusti Fawcett, Scarlett Fever, Selina Kyle, Shae Shae LaReese, Shealita Babay, Shugah Caine, Stephanie Roberts, Stephanie Stuart, Stormy Vain, Summer Breeze, Sybil Storm, Tabatha Lovall, Tatum Michelle, Teri Courtney, Tiffani Middlesexx, Timm McBride, Toni Davyne, TotiYanah Diamond,Trixie LaRue, Trixie Pleasures, Vegas Platinum, Venus D Lite, Vivika D'Angelo, Wendel Duppert and Wendy G. Kennedy.

Book 3:   DRAG411's
"Crown Me! Winning Pageants"

Hundreds of invitations sent to the titleholders, pageant promoters, judges, and talent show hosts to share their insight on not only winning pageants and contests but also owning the stage every time they perform. Their topics included auxiliary steps to success needed for song selection, dancing, movement onstage, props, backup dancers, creating your own edge, personal interviews, steps to success for winning the talent category every time you step onstage, onstage questions, eveningwear, and creative costuming. They discussed in their own unedited words, wardrobe changes, makeup, hair, shoes, when is the time to compete, qualities needed for a judge, and the top misconceptions of contestants competing in the pageantry systems.

Commentary shared with Todd Kachinski Kottmeier included the following contributors of Crown Me! to include AJ Menendez, Amy DeMilo, Anastacia Dupree, Anson Reign, Bob Taylor, Breonna Tenae, Brittany T Moore, Coco Montrese, Dana Douglas, Darryl Kent, Denise Russell, Dey Jzah Opulent, Freddy Prinze Charming, Gage Gatlyn, Jay Santana , Jayden Knight, Jennifer Foxx, Joey Jay, Kori Stevens, Mis Sadistic, Mykul Jay Valentine, Natasha Richards, Rico Taylor, Sam Hare, Stephanie Stuart, Taina T. Norell, Tiffani Middlesexx, Tori Taylor, Ty Nolan, Vinnie Marconi, and Vivika D'Angelo.

Book 4:   DRAG411's
"DRAG King Guide"

Over 155 male impersonators around the world share over a thousand insightful comments in forty-one chapters.

Commentary shared with Todd Kachinski Kottmeier included the following contributors of The Official DRAG King and Male Impersonators Guide to include Aaron Phoenix, Abs Hart, Adam All, Adam DoEve, AJ Menendez, Alec Allnight, Alexander Cameron, Alik Muf, Andrew Citino, Anjie Swidergal, Anson Reign, Ashton The Adorable Lover, Atown, Ayden Layne, B J Armani, B J Bottoms, Bailey Saint James, Ben Doverr, Ben Eaten, Bootzy Edwards Collynz, Brandon KC Young-Taylor-Taylor, Bruno Diaz, Cage Masters, Campbell Reid Andrews, Chance Wise, Chandler J Hart, Chasin Love, Cherry Tyler Manhattan, Chris Mandingo, Clark Kunt, Clint Torres, Cody Wellch Klondyke,

Colin Grey, Corey James Caster, Coti Blayne, Crash Bandikok, Dakota Rain, Dante Diamond, Davion Summers, DeVery Bess, Devin G. Dame, Devon Ayers, Dionysus W Khaos, Diseal Tanks Roberts, D-Luv Saviyon, Dominic Demornay, Dominic Von Strap, D-Rex, Dylan Kane, E. M. Shaun, Eddie C. Broadway, Emilio, Erick LaRue, Flex Jonez, Freddy Prinze Charming, Gabe King, Gage Gatlyn, George De Micheal, Greyson Bolt, Gunner Gatlyn, Gus Magendor, Hawk Stuart, Harry Pi, Holden Michael, Howie Feltersnatch, Hurricane Savage, J Breezy St James, Jack E. Dickinson, Jack King, Jake Van Camp, Jamel Knight, Jenson C. Dean, Johnnie Blackheart, Jonah Godfather of DRAG, Jordan Allen, Jordan Reighn, Joshua K. Mann, Joshua Micheals, Juan Kerr, Julius M. SeizeHer, Jude Lawless, Justin Cider, Justin Luvan, Justin Sider, K'ne Cole, Kameo Dupree, Kenneth J. Squires, King Dante, King Ramsey, Jack Inman, Kody Sky, Koomah, Kristian Kyler, Kruz Mhee, Linda Hermann-Chasin, Luke Ateraz, Lyle Love-It, Macximus, Marcus Mayhem, Marty Brown, Master Cameron Eric Leon, Max Hardswell, MaXx Decco, Michael Christian, Mike Oxready, Miles Long, Mr-Charlie Smith, Nanette D'angelo Sylvan, Nolan Neptune, Orion Blaze Browne, Owlejandro Monroe, Papa Cherry, Papi Chulo, Papi Chulo Doll, Persian Prince, Phantom, Pierce Gabriel, Rasta Boi Punany, Rico M Taylor, Rock McGroyn, Rocky Valentino, Rogue DRAG King, Romeo Sanchez, Rychard "Alpha" Le'Sabre, Ryder Knightly, Ryder Long, Sam Masterson, Sammy Silver, Santana Romero, Scorpio, Shane Rebel Caine, Shook ByNature, Silk Steele Prince, SirMandingo Thatis, Smitty O'Toole, Soco Dupree, Spacee Kadett, Starr Masters, Stefan LeDude, Stefon Royce Iman, Stefon SanDiego, Stormm, Teddy Michael, Thug Passion, Travis Luvermore, Travis Hard, Trey C. Michaels, Trigger Montgomery, Tyler Manhattan, Viciouse Slick, Vinnie Marconi, Welland Dowd, William Vanity Matrix, Wulf Von Monroe, Xander Havoc, and Xavier Bottoms.

Book 5:   DRAG411's
"DRAG Stories"

Funny stories shared with Todd Kachinski Kottmeier including the following contributors of DRAG Stories to include Chance Wise, Anson Reign, Tiffani Middlesexx, Rico Taylor, Todd Kachinski Kottmeier, Bob Taylor, Stefon Royce Iman, Candi Samples, Alexis Mateo, Naomi Wynters, Dmentia Divinyl, Bruce Lacie, Kennedy Wendy, Chastity Rose, Miss GiGi, Angel gLamar, Patricia Grand, Shook ByNature, Lady Guy, Eunyce Raye, Charley Marie Coutora, Jezzie Bell, Lamar Kellam, Jayden St. James, Rachelle Ann Summers, Champagne T Bordeaux, Gilda Golden, Daisha Monet, Vivika D'Angelo, Rachel Boheme, Esme Rodriguez, and MaNu Da Original.

Book 6:   DRAG411's
"DRAG Mother, DRAG Father" Honoring Mentors

Performers look to DRAG mothers, DRAG fathers, friends, and fans for insight, compassion, and guidance as mentors. This book honors those special people. Over 140 entertainers contributed wisdom and words for this historical book, making it the largest project of its nature in GLBTQ history and the first published book on male and female mentors.

Commentary shared with Todd Kachinski Kottmeier included the following contributors of DRAG Parents to includee AJ Menendez, Vinnie Marconi, Mis Sadistic, Todd Kachinski Kottmeier, Bob Taylor, Taina Norell, Andrew Stratton, Horchata Horchata, VIKKI SHOKK, Gianna Love, Trinity Taylor, Domunique Jazmin Vizcaya, Brittany Moore, PurrZsa Kyttyn, Jake Lickus, Shelita Taylor, Adriana Manchez, MiMi Welch, China Taylor, Armondis Bone't, Monique Trudeau, Simeon Codfish, Diamond Dupree, Stefon Royce Iman, Jayden Stjames, Demonica da Bomb, Colin Grey, Christopher Todd Guy, Celyndra Lashay Clyne, Candice St. James, Justin Barnes Williams, Ivanna Dooche, London Taylor Douglas, Christina Alexandria Victoria Regina Lowe, Bianca DeMonet, Critiqa Mann, Jazmen Andrews, AJ Allen, TotiYanah Diamond, D' Marco Knight, Chip Matthews, Mirage Montrese, India Starr Simms, Jade S Stratton, Emerald Divine, Elysse Giovanni, Vanity Halston, Kristofer Reynolds, Akasha

Uravitch, Adriana Fuentes, Erykah Mirage, Felicity Ferraro, Joey Payge, Rhiannon Todd, Vicious Slick, Amirage Saling, Tori Sass, Chy'enne Valentino, and Robbi Lynn.

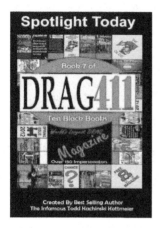

Book 7:   DRAG411's
"Spotlight Today"

It was the World's Largest Paperback Magazine for Impersonators and Fans when it premiered with over 175 pages. DRAG411 no longer prints Spotlight Today Magazine, but here is the re-release of the groundbreaking first edition. Complete articles by Vinnie Marconi, Denise Russell, Tiffani T. Middlesexx, Kristofer Reynolds, Magenta Alexandria Dupree, Butch Daddy, Vivikah Kayson-Raye, Makanoe, Amanda Lay, Thomas DeVoyd, Kevin B. Reed, Glenn Storm, and over 150 impersonators from around the world.

Book 8:   DRAG411's
"DRAG Queen Guide"

Almost two hundred female impersonators around the world share over a thousand insightful comments in forty-one chapters.

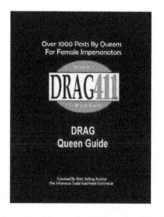

Almost two hundred female impersonators around the world share over a thousand insightful comments in forty-one chapters. Commentary shared with Todd Kachinski Kottmeier included the following contributors: Alana Summers, Alexis Marie Von Furstenburg, Alize', Aloe Vera, Alysin Wonderland, Amanda Bone DeMornay, Amanda Lay, Amanda Roberts, Amy DeMilo, Anastasia Fallon, Angie Ovahness, Anita Mandinite, Appolonia Cruz, Ashlyn Tyler, Aurora Tr'Nele Michelle, Azia Sparks, Barbie Dayne, Barbra Herr, Beverly LaSalle, Bianca DeMonet, Bianca Lynn Breeze, Blair Michaels, Boxxa Vine, Brandi Amara Skyy, Britney Towers, Brittany T Moore, Brooke Lynn Bradshaw, Candi Samples, Candi Stratton, Candy Sugar, Cathy Craig, Catia Lee Love, CeCe Georgia , Cee-Cee LaRouge-Avalon, Celeste Starr, Chad Michaels, Chevon Davis, Cheyenne Desoto Mykels, Chi Chi Lalique, Christina Collins, Chrystal Conners, Claudia B Eautiful, Coca Mesa, Coco St James, Damiana LaRoux, Dana Scrumptious, Danyel Vasquez, Dee Gregory, Delores T. Van-Cartier, Demonica DaBaum, Denise Russell, Diamond Dunhill, Diva Lilo, Diva Savage, Dove, EdriAna Treviño, Elle Emenopé, Elysse Giovanni, Erica James, Esmé Rodríguez, Estella Sweet, Eunyce Raye, Eva Nichole Distruction, Faleasha Savage, Felicia Minor, Felicity Frockaccino, Gigi Masters, Ginger Alley, Ginger Gigi Diamond, Ginger Kaye Belmont, Glitz Glam, Grecia Montes D' Occa, Heather Daniels, Hennessy Heart, Hershae Chocolatae, Holy McGrail, Hope B Childs, Horchata, India Brooks, India Ferrah, Ivy Profen, Izzy Adahl, Jaclyn St James, Jade Iroq, Jade Sotomayor, Jade Taylor Stratton, Jamie-Ree Swan, Jennifer Warner, Jessica Brooks, Jexa Ren'ae Van de Kamp, Joey Brooks, Jonny Pride, Kamden T. Rage, Kamelle Toe, Karma Jayde Addams, Kelly Turner, Kira Stone-St James, Kirby Kolby, Kita Rose, Krysta Radiance, Lacie Bruce, Lady Jasmine Michaels, Lady Pearl, Lady Sabrina, LaTonga Manchez, Latrice Royale, Leona Barr, Lexi

Alexander, Lilo Monroe, Lindsay Carlton, Lucinda Holliday, Lunara Sky, Lupita Chiquita Michaels   Alexander, Madam Diva Divine, Mahog Anny, Makayla Michelle Davis Diamond, Mama Savannah Georgia, Mariah Cherry, Maxine Padlock, Melody Mayheim, Menaje E'toi, Mercede Andrews, Mi$hal, Mia Fierce, Michelle Leigh Sterling, Miss Diva Savage, Miss GiGi, Misty Eyez, Mitze Peterbilt, Monica Mystique, Montrese Lamar Hollar, Morgana DeRaven, Mr. Kenneth Blake, Muffy Vanbeaverhousen, Natasha Richards, Nathan Loveland, Nicole Paige Brooks, Nikki Garcia, Nostalgia Todd Ronin, Olivia St James, Paige Sinclair, Pandora DeCeption, Pheobe James, Reia'Cheille Lucious, Rhonda Sheer, Robyn Demornay, Robyn Graves, Rose Murphy, Ruby Diamond NY, Ruby Holiday, Ryan Royale, Rychard "Alpha" Le'Sabre, Rye Seronie, Sable Monay, Sabrina Kayson-Raye, Samantha St Clair, Sanaa Raelynn, Sapphire T. Mylan, Sasha Phillips, Savannah Rivers, Savannah Stevens, Selina Kyle, Sha'day Halston-St James, ShaeShae LaReese, Shamya Banx, Shana Nicole, Shaunna Rai, Sierra Foxx White, Sierra Santana, Sonja Jae Savage, Stella D'oro, Strawberry Whip, Sugarpill, Tanna Blake, Taquella Roze, Tasha Carter, Tawdri Hipburn, Taylor Rockland, Tempest DuJour, Tiffani T. Middlesexx, Traci Russell, Trudy Tyler, Vanessa del Rey, Velveeta WhoreMel, Vera Delmar, Vicky Summers, Vita DeVine, Vivian Sorensin, Vivian Von Brokenhymen, Vivika D'Angelo-Steele, Wendy G. Kennedy, Willmuh Dickfit, Wynter Storm, Yasmine Alexander, and ZuZu Bella.

Book 9:   DRAG411's (Two Comedy Scripts)
"Best Said Dead" and **"Following Wynter"**

Best Said Dead examines in funny conversations those brief minutes after a person dies. Many religions and beliefs define different paths for each of us. Rarely do we discuss those precious moments between death and the final destination. This comedy opens the possibilities that for a moment, a person vanishes into the memories in their mind. Any part can be male, female, or ambiguous.

Following Wynter is a hilarious comedy play. Ethan discovers his newlywed husband is the flamboyant DRAG Queen Wynter Storm in this whimsical farce with an important message of believing in yourself and your friends. . . even if your friend is Serena Silver. Any part can be male, female, or ambiguous.

Book 10:   DRAG411's
"DRAG World"
The contributing writers of DRAG411's "Spotlight Magazine," the World's Largest Paperback Magazine for Impersonators and Fans when it premiered in 2012 with over 175 pages, created this companion book. DRAG411 no longer prints Spotlight Today Magazine, but above you will find Book 7 is the re-release of the groundbreaking first edition. Complete chapters on DRAG Marketing by DRAG411.

Complimentary articles on Confidence, Duct Tape, Music Selection, Living Divinely, authentic stage presence, Pageants, having fun performing, jewelry, legislative information from the United States and around the world, the Old School performers, Virgin stage performers, and payday from contributing writers including Denise Russell, Jay Santana, Chance Wise, Vivikah Kayson-Raye, AJ Menedez,

Who's Who of DRAG

Glenn Storm, Freddy Prinze Charming, Gage Gatlyn, Kevin B. Reed, and over 100 impersonators from around the world!

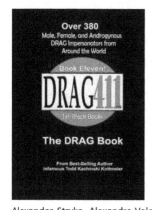

Over 380
Male, Female, and Androgynous
DRAG Impersonators from
Around the World

Book Eleven!

DRAG411

Ten Black Books

The DRAG Book

From Best-Selling Author
Infamous Todd Kachinski Kottmeier

Book 11: DRAG411's
"The DRAG Book"
Ten books, that was supposed to be the challenge when the publisher was diagnosed with onset dementia, but the Infamous Todd Kachinski Kottmeier knew he could challenge himself to document a few more DRAG stories and lessons. This is hundreds and hundreds of performers sharing their advice to performers across the world through over fifty questions.

Commentary shared with Todd Kachinski Kottmeier included the following contributors A'ryiah Monè Diamond, Aaliyah Tealheart, Abs Hart, ADHD, Adriana Manchez, Adriana Mariee Kardashh, Aero Dean, Afro~Deity, Alexander Moonwalker Knightly Jackson, Alexander Stryke, Alexandre Valentino Skye, Alexandro Rox, Alexis De La Mer, Alexis Milan, Alexis von Furstenberg, Alexye'us Paris, Allie Waye, Amadeus X Machina, Amanda Bone DeMornay, Amanda D Rhod, Amanda Playwith, Ambrosia S Thorne, Amy DeMilo, Andrea Forwards Anhedonia Delight, Anitta Schwanz, Aniya Stars, AnnaStaysha, Anne Drogyny, Ariana Autumn, Ariana Love, Astara Love, Auda Beaux Di, Aura Glitz, Aurora F. Sterling, Aurora LeKohl, Aurora Nicole, Aurora Risay, Aurora Veil, Autumn Holiday, Avery Rose Norwood, Azaria Kimberly Vallium, Barbie Dayne, Barbie Dicks, Barbra Herr, Bearonce Bear, Beau D. Vyne Bianca Blak, Bianca L'Amour Billy Jean, BinKyee Bellflower, BJ Bottoms, Blair Which, Blu Shady, Blyss Carrington, Bonni Blake, Bran Ray Lavo, Brandon KC Young-Taylor, Brandon Race, Brendan Bravado, Brock Harder, Bronzie De'Marco Bubonic Rose, Buttwiser, Cake Moss, Candie Hearts, Candy Buttons, Carly Uninemclite, Carmen Love, Carnelian Clinique Carnita Asada, Carter Bachmann, Casanova, Cass Marie Domino, Catastrophē Nicole Knight, Cathy Craig, CC, Charlie Mornett von Trash, Chase Sky, Cher Michaels, Cheri Bomb LeKohl, Cherilyn Matthews, Chevelle Chardonnay, Chiffon Dior, Christian Mingle, Christina Collins, Christopher Allure, Christopher Peterson, Clara Tea, Colin Grey, Crystal Blu, CupCake, Daisy May, Dani Panic, Danilo De la Torre, Danyel Vasquez, Daphnie Moonwalker Rains, Deandra Dee Paige, Dee Dee Van Carter, DeeDee Marie Holliday, Deja Van Cartier, Delores T. Van-Cartier, Demona Frost, Denise Russell, Derek Skye Villaverde, Desiree DeMornay Destinē Brookes, Destiny B, Childs, Diego Wolf, Diva Kingsley, Diva Lilo, Diva Savage, Dizzy Grant Diamandis, D-Luv Saviyon, Dolly Bee Wellington, Donny Mirassou, Dovey Diabolique, Dr. Rasta Boi Punany, Dre Seymour-Mykals, Dunkin Dame, Dymond Onasis, Eazy Love Eddie Edwards, Edna D Mascará, Eileen Taylor Elle Taylor, Elyce Michaels, Erica St, Michaels, Erotica Romance, Estella Sweet, Eunice Alexander, Eva Dystruction, Evian Waters, Evona Valentino James, Felicia Minor, Felicity Foxhaven, Fiera Ice, Flame E Morning-Star DeMornay, Frank Lee, Frothy La Frou Frou, Galaxÿ, GatorDunn, Genevee Ramona Love, Gina D'licious, Ginger Beer, Gorgina George, Gyp'C Royal, Harpy Daniels, Hazel Derèon, Helena Handbasket Helix Rider, Henni C, Hershae Chocolatae, Holly Louya, Hunta Downe, Hunter Downs Morgan, Ian Syder-Blake, Idina Rimes, Imani Valentino, Iris Fay Moonwalker, irishimo, Ivana B, Real, Ivy League, Jade DeVere, JaJa Ohmai Whoremoans, James Cass, Jamie Cole, Jamie Monroe, Jasmine Skyy, Jason Beauregard, JC Rios, Jenna Starr, Jennifer Foxx, Jennifer Lynn, Jessica Deveraux, Jessica L'Whor, Jessica Patterson, Joanna James, Jodie Santana, Joey Brooks, Joey Gallagher, Josie Purée, Justice Twist, Justin Deeper-Love, Justyn Caze, Juuls, Kade Jackwell, Kahtya Tehnsion, KaiKai Bee Michaels, Kaleigha Diamond, Kamden T. Rage, Kandi Dishe, Kara Belle, Kathryn Nevets, Kay Fierce, KayKay Lavelle Kelasia Karmikal, KHAOS, Ki'Arra Infiniti-Ross, KiKi Mamah, King Blaze Khrystian, King Chris Dingo, King Crimson, King Perka $exxx , Kitt Raven, Kitty Litter Konstance Panic, Kruz Mhee, Krystal Cain, Krystal Cassadine, Krystal Naomi, Kyla G'Diva

Who's Who of DRAG

Rogue, Lacie Bruce, Lady Cynthia, Lady Inferno Diamond, Lady Sabrina, Lady Seduca, Ladycat De'Ore, Lamia - The Cursed Queen, LeKross DeAire Menendez, Leota Tombs, Lethia Dose, Liam Axel, Liquor Mini, Logan Rider, London Divine Sinclaire, Lori Divine, Luci Furr-Matrix, Lucy Paradisco LUST, M.C. Rawr, Madam D, Madame Fellatia Monroe, Makayla Rose Devine, MaKayla Styles, Martini, Matt Cockrin, Maxum Delray, Melissa Mason, Melody Lush, Mia Inez Adams, Michael Kane, Miles N. Sider Austin Mischa Michaels Miss Conception, Miss Domeaner MorningStar, Miss Piss, Molly Mormen, Momma Ashley Rose, Momma, Mona Lotz, Monique Michaels-Alexander, Morgan Davis, Morgana de Luxe, Mr. Killin Ya Softly, Muffy Rosenberg, Muni Tox, Mystique Summers, Naomi DeMornay, Natalie L. Carter, Nick D'Cuple, Nicole DuBois, Nikki Ontolodge Monet, Nikki Saxx, Nikki Silva, Nikoli Popov, Norma Llyaman, Oliver Steerpike, Ophelia Bottoms, Ophelia Handful, Osiris Romanov, Paisley Parque, Pandora DeStrange, Parris B. Cbello, Patrice Knight, Patricia Del Rosario, Patricia Mason, Patty Cakes, Paula Jenkins, PheYonce Montrese Pierce Gabriel, Piranha Del Rey Porsha DeMarco Douglas, Preston Steamed, Prince Kodhi Black Khrystian, Prince Silk St, James, Prinze Valentino, PurrZsa Kyttyn Azrael, Queen Issa Fella, Ramona Mirage, Ravion Starr Alexandria St James, Reba MacIntosh, Rebel Rose, Red Scare, Redd FaFilth, Renita Valdez, Richard La Petite, Rico Taylor, Robyn Hearts, Rockell Blu, Romeo Casanova, Romonica DiGregory, Rouge Fatale, Royale Payne, Ruby James Knight, Sally West, Salma Love Taylor, Sanaa Raelynn, Saniya Chanel Iman, Santana Romero, Sapphire Mylan, Sasha Turrelle, Sassy Sascha, Saylor Alexander Vontrell, Sean Wolff, Senpai, Serra Tonan Savage, ShaeShae LaReese, Shane West, Shasta McNastie, Shaunna Rai, Shelita Taylor, Shire Paige, Sho Sho Zahav, Sina Kakes, Sir Labia Sister Alphena Omega, Skarlet Overkill, Soluna LaVie-Mason Spring Summers, St. Reign, Staci Sings, Starr Shine, Stephanie Stuart, Sue Purr Nova, Suga Avery Bottoms, Sugar Vermonte, Sunny Banks Zane Paige, Sylas Crow, Talia Secret, Tank TopOff, Tara Nicole Brooks, Tara Shay Montgomery, Taylor Dame, Teri Lovo, Teri Taylor, Tia Douglas, Tierra Stone, Tina Louise, Tommy Boy, Tova Ura Vitch, Traynbow, Treasure Rose, Trixie Deflair, Trixy Valentine, Tucker Bleu, Tucker Downtown, Tuesdae Knyte, Twila Starr, Valentino Rose, Valerie Rockwell, Vera DelMar, Veranda L'Ni, Veronica Fox, Veronica Sledge, Versage, Vicki Vincent, Victoira Styles, Victoria Michaels, Victoria Obvious Queen, VIKKI SHOKK, Vinnie Marconi, Vintage Blue, Vivian Von Brokenhymen, Vivika D'Angelo Steele, VonScene, Vyki Z LaRoxx, Wanda Wheeler, Wendy G. Kennedy, Willy Hardt, Xander Morgan Valentine, Xavier Bottoms, Xiomarie LaBeija, Zoe Bitters, and Zoey Zegai.

Coming Autumn 2022
Book 12
DRAG SHOW
What it takes to get on stage

Made in the USA
Monee, IL
17 June 2022

98200322R00115